Gwynedd
The Shame of Britain

CREDITS

WRITTEN BY

Mark Shirley

EDITING

Carol Johnson

PROOF READING

Alexandra James

DESIGN AND LAYOUT

The Design Mechanism

ARTISTS

James Turpin, Colin Driver, Dean Spencer

PLAYTESTERS

Graham Blake, Ali Clamp, Camo Coffey, Mike Rudd, and Neil Rutherford. Thanks to Sarah Coffey for her Welsh language assistance.

FIND US AT

www.thedesignmechanism.com and *www.mythrasrpg.com*.
Facebook: *https://www.facebook.com/The-Design-Mechanism*

CONTENTS

Introduction	3
History of the Region	3
Clan Einion	7
Members	7
Allies and Enemies	9
Clan Ceredig	1
Members	1
Allies and Enemies	2
Secrets	2
Clan Osfael	5
Members	5
Allies and Enemies	15
Secrets	16
The Venedoti	17
Members	17
Allies and Enemies	18
Other Factions	20
Gwaelod	20
Powys	20
Siluria	21
Blackshield Irish	21
Druids and Priests	22
Places	23
Encounters	25
Quarrelling Princes	27
Gwynedd Campaigns	41
The Coat of Beisrydd	41
The Flooding of Maes Gwyddno	41
The Madness of Ynys Mon	42
The Head of Bran the Blessed	46
Appendices: Maps & Pronunciation	50

Mythras is a trademark of The Design Mechanism.
All rights reserved. This edition of Mythic Britain: Gwynedd is copyright © 2023. This book may not be reproduced in whole or in part by any means without permission from The Design Mechanism, except as quoted for purposes of illustration, discussion, and game play. Reproduction of the material in this book for the purposes of personal or corporate profit, by photographic, electronic, or other methods of retrieval is strictly prohibited.

For details of the Mythras Gateway license, please contact The Design Mechanism (designmechanism@gmail.com).

INTRODUCTION

Mythic Britain: Gwynedd is a mini-campaign that explores a world of warring factions within the Kingdom of Gwynedd in northwest Wales.

The campaign concerns the war-torn land of Gwynedd, a setting where faction politics are of premier importance. The rival clans of Einion and Ceredig are fighting bitterly for control over the Kingdom of Gwynedd; if they cannot settle the war soon, then it may be too late for either faction to win.

Given the importance of these two clans, Mythic Britain: Gwynedd uses the rules found in *Mythras Factions*. These rules allow the Games Master to track the progress of the plots and schemes of a number of different political groups in the game world, as well as measure their success against one another. Access to this supplement is highly recommended.

The campaign rounds out with stories set in Gwynedd that make full use of the Faction rules and presented setting.

HISTORY OF THE REGION

BEFORE CUNEDDA

Two tribes occupied Gwynedd before the Romans came: the Gangani in the west and the Deceangi in the east, an offshoot of the Gangani who had mingled their blood with an Ordovices clan. The region was known as Guinet or Gwynedd, which mutated into "Venedotia" in the mouths of the Roman conquerors. Venedotia had a heavy Roman presence, and Romans ruthlessly suppressed the native tribes. In the year 61, Paulinus lead the massacre of the British druids, who had met in congress on Ynys Mon. Since that date, no Briton has set foot on the island and returned unchanged, save, perhaps, Merlin.

 **FACTIONS PROGRESS**

The scores of the goals of Gwynedd's factions are currently unspecified. The Games Master is free to determine them as they see fit. Some of the goals might be near completion, or the last 20 years could have seen so many missions and counter-missions that little progress has been made.

By the time the Romans withdrew from Britain, the Gangani and Deceangi had joined into a single tribe informally called the Venedoti. They re-established their pre-conquest kingdoms of Lleyn (made up of the current cantrefs of Afflogion, Arfon, and Dunodion) and Rhos (contemporary Rhos, Rhufoniog, and Dogfeilion). The monarchs of these two kingdoms shared a single royal family; indeed, the kings were often brothers. or father and son. Between them, the two kings agreed on a crown prince, who would assume whichever throne became vacant first.

The fertile valleys and gold-rich mountains of Gwynedd became attractive to those displaced from their own homelands. First the Irish and the Manx came, then the Silures. The land was beset and its people under siege. The last Venedoti king of Lleyn was Tudwal; his eldest son Cynfawr was the king of Rhos and the crown prince was Cynfawr's brother Dylan Traws. These three leaders of Gwynedd were fighting a losing battle against the invaders, who were squabbling over Gwynedd like dogs over scraps. However, it was a tribe of Votadini Picts from Northern Britain who finally seized the prize, led by a man called Cunedda.

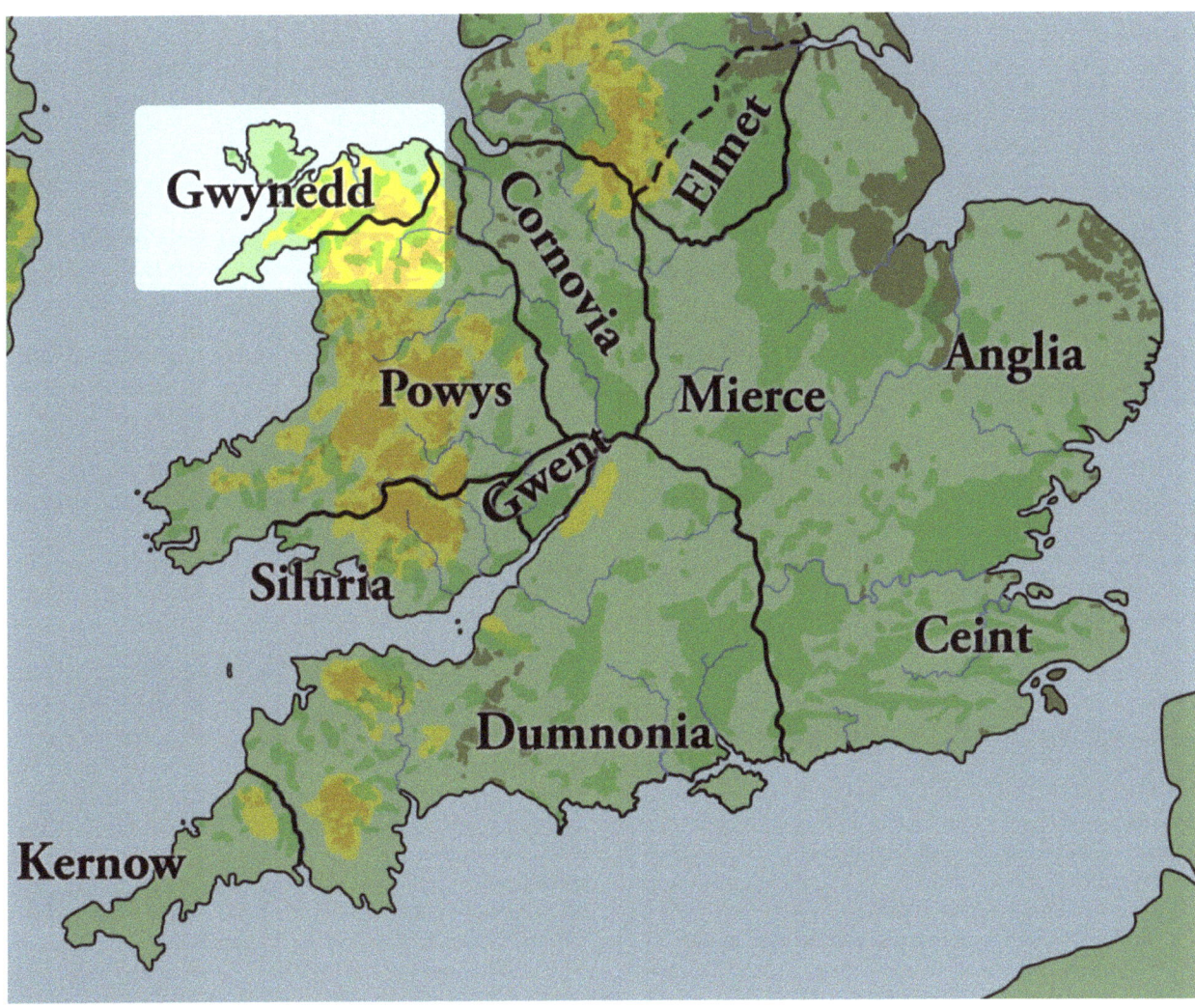

CONQUEST BY THE PICTS

Cunedda was a warlord who served under King Culdh of Gododdin. When Lot ap Lein slew Culdh and seized control of the Votadini, he and Cunedda clashed violently. Rather than exterminate his clan in a pointless feud against a stronger opponent, Cunedda set his eyes on other goals. About 50 years ago, he came to Gwynedd with his son Typaun and infant grandson Meirion, along with a host of warriors. His reason for coming specifically to Gwynedd is unclear, although his early campaigns against the Irish seemed to target gaining control over Ynys Mon. However, his ambitions in this direction abruptly ended when Typaun returned from the island raving mad.

It took Cunedda five years to bring Gwynedd to its knees. He drove out the invaders and demanded homage from the natives, slaying their chiefs if they refused. He cemented his kingship by taking three additional wives, each of them the daughter of a prominent British chieftain. He encouraged his Pictish followers to follow his example, rewarding each one who took a British wife with a chiefdom.

Cunedda ruled Gwynedd for 20 years and had eight more sons with his British wives. Perhaps encouraged by the antipathy between their mothers, the sons were forever in competition for their father's attention. Despite Ceredig being the most accomplished, it was clear that Einion was the most favoured. When Ceredig accused Einion of raping his wife, Cunedda ruled in favour of Einion's innocence, citing Aula's promiscuous reputation as his justification. The incensed Ceredig publicly insulted his father and was exiled; he left Gwynedd and won fame as a warlord in service to Powys.

UNCIVIL WAR

Before Cunedda died, he split his kingdom into nine portions, or cantrefs: one for each of his sons, with Meirion receiving the portion due to his deceased father Typaun. However, Cunedda denied the exiled Ceredig his birthright and instead

a double share was given to Cunedda's favourite son Einion. Cunedda decreed the next king of Gwynedd would be whichever of his sons had the unanimous support of the other princes. He hoped this partitioning of his kingdom would lead one strong leader to rise — either a warlord who could conquer his enemies or a diplomat who could unite the warring provinces. Either way, his dynasty would be in safe hands.

Some of the princes were dissatisfied with the partitioning of Gwynedd, and after Cunedda's death, called for Ceredig to return and rule as king of Gwynedd. In response, Einion made a claim to the throne himself, supported by his brothers Rhwfon, Afloyg, and Dogfeil. The stalemate between the Einionydd (who supported Einion) and the Ceredigydd (who supported Ceredig) lasted for seven years. When Ceredig finally returned to Gwynedd, he did so with an army at his back mustered from his new lands in Powys. He was joined by his brothers Dynod and Ederyn, and his nephew Meirion. They were met by the alliance lead by Einion, and a mighty battle ensued near the shores of Llyn Tegid. Many famous warriors of Gwynedd died that day, including three of Cunedda's sons: Ceredig killed Einion, Deithlyn (Einion's father-in-law) killed Ceredig, and Meirion killed Rhwfon.

The northern Einionydd were later judged the winner, but on the day, they failed to press the advantage they achieved. Meirion lead his uncle's armies back south where he was acclaimed Ceredig's successor and leader of the Ceredigydd, being substantially older than either of the brothers of Ceredig who had supported him. Meanwhile in the Einionydd, Deithlyn became regent for his grandsons Cadwallon and Owain ap Einion, After Cadwallon inherited Afflogion from his childless uncle, the clan deemed the young prince old enough to rule the Einionydd in his own right and he formally received homage from Dogfeil and Benlli ap Rhwfon. He shares the leadership of the clan with his younger brother Owain, and they each rule one of their father's two cantrefs.

While neither clan was willing to relinquish its claim over Gwynedd, both were heavily depleted by the fighting. The hostilities de-escalated from open warfare to one of attrition, raiding, and guerrilla action. It is still simmering 22 years later.

THE OAKEN TORC OF GWYNEDD

A rope of twisted gold, decorated with oak leaves, is the ancient symbol of Gwynedd, prior even to Cunedda's conquest. It is symbolic of the kingship of the land. Cunedda was the last to wear the torc, and it currently lies on top of his tomb under Caer Segeint waiting for the next king of Gwynedd to wear it around his neck.

Cunedda decreed three conditions were required to succeed him. To be eligible to be king, the candidate must be both a blood-descendant of Cunedda and rule at least one of Gwynedd's cantrefs. To receive the torc of kingship, the individual must also be unopposed by all other eligible candidates. Cunedda wanted a strong leader to succeed him: one who could gain the alliance of all the other princes, subjugate them on the field of battle, or be ruthless enough to eliminate all competition.

CUNEDDA'S WIVES

Some would say the cause of the grief that lays upon Gwynedd is Cunedda's four wives, with the sons of Einid and Gwawl united against the sons of Meredith and Olwen.

Einid was Cunedda's first wife and a full blooded Pict. They had been married for 30 years by the time Cunedda moved to Gwynedd, and their son Typaun already had a wife and children of his own. Typaun also had numerous sisters who had been married off to Votadini chieftains, some of whom accompanied Cunedda to Gwynedd and some who remained in Gododdin.

Olwen was the first of Cunedda's British wives, the daughter of King Tudwal of Lleyn. After he killed her father and brother, Cunedda raped Olwen and then forced her into marriage after she bore him a son, Osfael. Olwen hated her husband and loathed the children he made her bear. After the birth of Afloyg, her second son and Cunedda's sixth, Olwen went truly mad and tried to murder her sister-wife Gwawl along with the baby she was carrying. Cunedda confined Olwen to Ynys Lannog, where she died a hermit. Cunedda's third wife Meredith fostered Osfael and Afloyg.

Meredith was from an Ordovices clan who had settled in the east of Gwynedd; her father was chief of Dinas Bran. She had three sons: Rhwfon (Cunedda's third son), Einion (Cunedda's seventh and favourite son), and Dogfeil (Cunedda's eighth son). Some have said Meredith was Cunedda's only love amongst his four wives; certainly Einid and Gwawl hate her. Meredith's offspring form the heart of the Einionydd.

Gwawl was Cunedda's fourth and youngest wife. Her father was a Gangani chief, perhaps the last one to survive the Roman purge. Her sons were Dynod (born fourth), Ceredig (born fifth), and Ederyn (born ninth and last). Gwawl's sons grew up with Einid's grandsons, and the two women grew very close.

 ## GWYNEDD'S FATE

Historically, the Einionydd defeated the Ceredigydd with the assistance of Powys, although Cadwallon Lawhir ap Einion dies in the fighting. His brother Owain Ddantgwyn became the first king of the reunited Gwynedd. King Owain is murdered in 517 by his nephew Maelgwyn ap Cadwallon who usurps the throne. Cadwallon exiles Owain's son Cynglas to Powys. According to Gildas and other period sources, both "Maglocunus" (Maelgwyn) and "Cuneglasus" (Cynglas) become High Kings of Britain after Arthur. Gildas, writing in 540, accuses both kings of moral depravity and holds them partially responsible for the "ruin of Britain." Despite this condemnation, the medieval kings of Gwynedd are proud to trace their lineage back to Maelgwyn and/or Cynglas.

CLAN EINION

The Einionydd is made up of the descendants of Cunedda and Meredith, his third wife. Meredith was a Christian, although her sons were raised pagan like their father. Einion had a dramatic conversion to the new faith, switching from being a violent thug and philandering libertine to living an almost ascetic existence. Where Einion led, his brothers, sons, and nephews followed, and the Einionydd is now almost entirely Christian.

The Einionydd currently rules the cantrefs of Arfon, Rhos, Rhufoniog, Dogfeilion, and Afflogion. Arfon and Rhos were the two cantrefs Einion inherited, and his two sons Cadwallon and Owain received one each. Afflogion was a deathbed behest from Afloyg to his nephew Cadwallon since the prince had no acknowledged heirs of his own. Cadwallon was only 15 at the time and was very close to his uncle — some say a little too close.

The main goals of the Einionydd are to wrest control of the rest of the cantrefs from Ceredigydd loyalists. They have been colluding with Eifion ap Dynod, brother of the current prince of Dunodion, to give him his brother's cantref in return for switching sides. Cadwallon also believes he can win over the neutral province of Osmaeliog, planning to use the close connection of their fathers to win over his cousin Elnaw. Meirionydd and Ederynion will have to be taken by force. The Einionydd has over twice the number of members than their rival faction, although most of them are young and untested.

If the clan has a flaw, it is weak leadership. All members of the faction are committed to the same cause, but each of the four princes holds the loyalty of his own men rather than serving under a single leader. Cadwallon and Owain are chiefs of the clan in name, but in truth the faction is run by committee and there is usually a great deal of negotiation needed to get anything done.

MEMBERS

The typical member of the Einionydd is a young, Christian chieftain in command of a small village fortified against the Irish and the Ceredigydd. The relative inexperience of the Einionydd may prove their undoing.

CADWALLON AP EINION

Cadwallon, nicknamed Lawhir ("Long Arm"), is the prince of Arfon and Afflogion. At just 25 years old, Cadwallon has a great deal of responsibility, not least an 8-year-old son Maelgwyn and three younger daughters. The handsome Cadwallon is a born leader. He is brave and intelligent, and strong with honour and faith. His biggest failing is his caution. He does not take risks, meticulously planning every detail.

OWAIN AP EINION

Nicknamed Ddantgwyn ("White Tooth"), Owain is the prince of Rhos and 3 years younger than his brother Cadwallon. Owain has a 4-year-old son Cynglas Goch and a 2-year-old son Einion. Owain is a slightly imperfect version of his brother — not as handsome, not as clever, and not as steadfast in his faith. While Cadwallon has always shared the leadership of the faction with him, Owain is aware that Cadwallon is the man to whom everyone looks, and that he is very much co-leader in name only. Owain spends a great deal of time with his grandfather Deithlyn, learning the art of a warrior and warleader; in this respect alone, he is better than his brother.

BENLLI AP RHWFON

The 28-year-old Prince of Rhufoniog stands virtually alone in the Einionydd in maintaining his pagan faith. His father Rhwfon was the last of his brothers to take the Cross; by the time he did, Benlli had already been fostered out to a pagan

CLAN EINION

Major Faction, Average Resources, Large Membership Size (2100 members), Moderate Dedication

Leaders
Cadwallon Lawhir and Owain Ddantgwyn

Cause
To Rule Gwynedd.

Faction Skills
Ally (Powys) 60%
Following 35%
Information 60%
Intrigue 55%
Subterfuge 40%

Goals
Stamp out the pagan faith in Gwynedd (public).
Regain control over Afflogion (public).
Install Eifion ap Dynod as Prince of Dunodion.
Gain support of Osmaeliog.
Conquer Meirionydd.
Conquer Ederynion.
Elect a descendent of Einion as King of Gwynedd (public).

household. He has since refused to abandon his faith in the gods. Despite this, Benlli is a strong supporter of the Einionydd cause and of Cadwallon in particular.

MOR AP RHWFON
Mor towers over all of his clan. He is not just tall, but broad as well; some jokingly call him "ap Gawr" (son of a giant), but he looks too much like his brother to be a bastard. Mor is a devout Christian and has personally built several chapels in Rhufoniog. Despite their different faiths, Mor and Benlli are close, although he has noticed recently that his older brother has become reserved and a little secretive.

DOGFEIL AP CUNEDDA
At 40 years old, the prince of Dogfeilion is the eldest of the two surviving sons of Cunedda. He is jealous of his nephews' popularity and resents the fact he is not in charge of the faction. He occasionally organises his own missions without consulting his fellow princes and these occasionally run counter to ongoing missions or the goals of the Einionydd. He is trying to prove himself, but the truth is that Dogfeil is neither clever nor inspiring enough to lead.

MEREDITH
The mother of Rhwfon, Einion, and Dogfeil, and very much the matriarch of the Einionydd. She maintains the alliance with Powys through her brother Madoc, who is the chief of Dinas Bran and loyal to King Cyngen. Meredith loves music, particularly singing.

PRAWST AN DEITHLYN
The wife of Einion and mother of Cadwallon and Owain. Meredith and Prawst are allies of convenience, but her Ordovices mother-in-law has never truly accepted her half-Pictish daughter-in-law, and as such, Prawst is very much overshadowed by Meredith.

DEITHLYN
A Pictish chieftain and Cunedda's warleader, Deithlyn accompanied his lord from Northern Britain. Deithlyn took a British wife and is the father of Prawst, Einion's widow. Deithlyn was a reluctant convert to Christianity, and he still occasionally calls upon his ancestor's gods out of reflex — Deithlyn is now approaching his seventh decade and is too old to undo the habits of a lifetime.

Allies and Enemies

Just as King Rhyddfedd of Powys supported Einion, so too does his son Cyngen support Cadwallon, providing troops and political pressure. Powys's assistance is less to do with the rightness of the Einionydd's claim and more to do with wanting a loyal Christian ally to the north of his kingdom.

The Einionydd have a hidden enemy in the Venedoti faction (page 17). This secret faction has insufficient resources to offer serious threat to the Einionydd, although it has been able to foil some of their plans without revealing its hand. The leader of the Venedoti would be king of Rhos had it not been for Cunedda, and this is the centre of their actions. The druid Afallach (page 22) is a public opponent of the Einionydd chiefs, but they assume that this is because of their Christian faith. The Einionydd seek covert ways of getting rid of him.

Secrets

Cadwallon's wife Meddyf is the daughter of Maeldaf, leader of the Venedoti. She was supposed to murder Cadwallon on their wedding night, but managed to convince her father that it would be better to wait until Owain could be neutralised first. In the meantime, she has given Cadwallon four children. Maeldaf is blind to the fact that his daughter is clearly in love with her husband, because he cannot conceive that one of his own kin would put personal happiness over familial duty. She has convinced Maeldaf that the adjustments to his plan were his ideas all along; Afallach knows the truth, but plans to use the threat of revelation to control his sister.

Benlli was raised in the household of Cendal, a British warlord and secretly the son of Cynfawr, the last British king of Rhos. The druid Afallach has persuaded Benlli that a Christian king should not wear Gwynedd's Oaken Torc, and Benlli is now convinced he is destined to wear the Oaken Torc. At the suggestion of his foster father, Benlli has begun to drive a wedge between Cadwallon and Owain, hoping to destabilise their alliance and giving himself an opportunity to seize control of the Einionydd.

When Ceredig accused Einion of raping his wife, he was telling the truth. Aula's son Gwyddno (page 11) is actually Einion's son, not Ceredig's. Cadwallon knows that the chief of Gwaelod is his half-brother rather than his cousin, and plans to use that fact to win Gwyddno over to his side. After all, they are both Christians, both sons of Einion, and both supported by Powys.

There is a rumour that Afloyg had an illegitimate son, who became a monk in Powys. This son would now be in his twenties, and if he had some proof of his descent from Cunedda, he could make a reasonable attempt to claim his father's principality from Cadwallon.

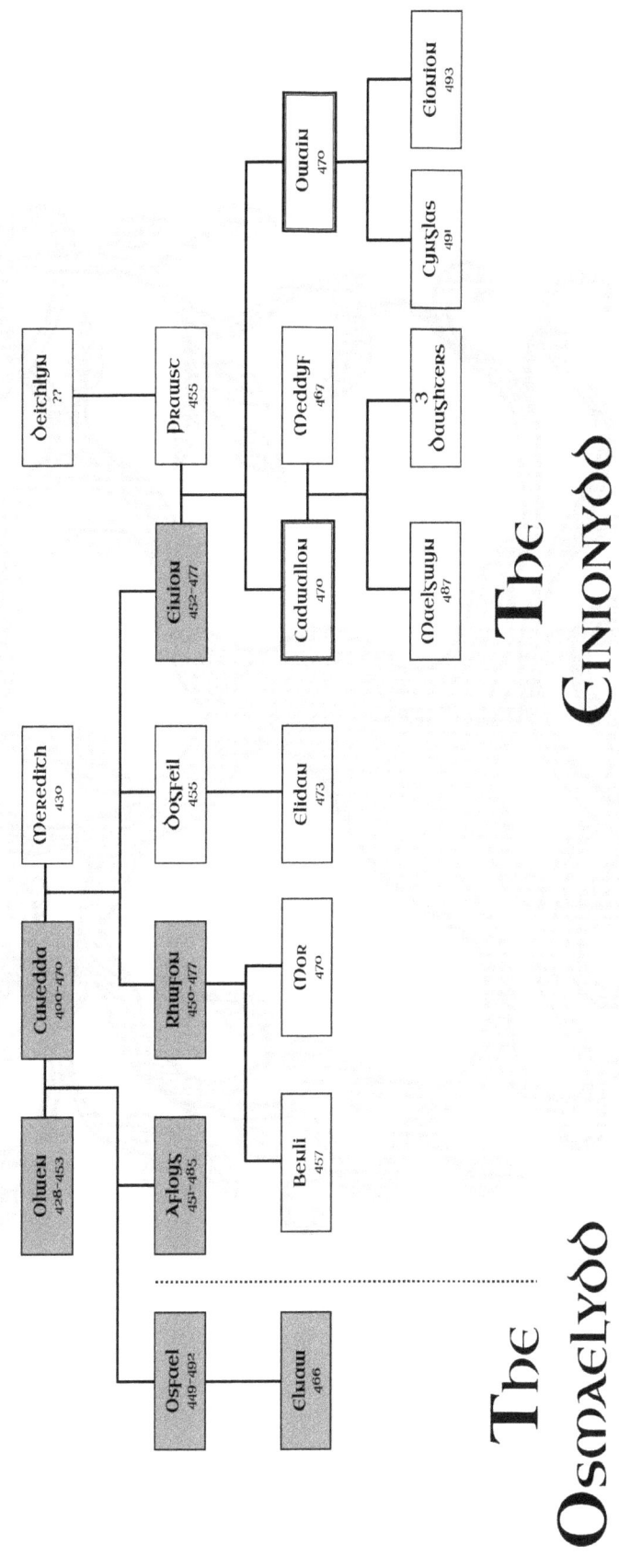

CLAN CEREDIG

When Ceredig made his attempt on Gwynedd's crown, his two full brothers Dynod and Ederyn supported him. Many of the Pictish chieftains who accompanied Cunedda from Northern Britain also supported Ceredig, mostly down to the efforts of Meirion, whose father Typaun was their war-leader. After Ceredig's death, Meirion was the natural choice for the leadership of his faction, and ever since the Einionydd began to purge its ranks of pagans, more have joined up with the Ceredigydd. The majority of the clan is pagan, although it has no druids who are active members.

Meirion and his kin dominate the Ceredigydd. With two brothers, three nephews, and two sons in the upper echelon of the faction, Meirion can command two thirds of the warriors himself. Add to this the dog-like loyalty of Ederyn towards Meirion and he controls three quarters of the faction. This is in contrast to the Einionydd, where leadership over the people is divided equally amongst four princes. Some believe Meirion has too much control; after all, it is meant to be Ceredig's faction yet the current leader is more distantly related to Ceredig than others of its membership. Some would prefer to put Ederyn or Dingad in control as more logical successors to Ceredig, or perhaps even Gwyddno — who is, after all, Ceredig's son (or so they believe; page 9). However, Gwyddno's Christian faith makes him an uncomfortable replacement for many.

MEMBERS

The Ceredigydd faction is smaller than its principal rival, although most of its members are older and more battle-hardened. The typical member is a middle-aged pagan warrior, usually with a Pictish or half-Pictish father. Most are tattooed in the Pictish style.

MEIRION AP TYPAUN AP CUNEDDA

The leader of Ceredig's clan is the 51-year-old prince of Meirionydd. He is a full-blooded Pict of the Votadini tribe, like his brothers Morvan and Morfran and their sons. Meirion's father was nearly 30 years older than any of his brothers and thus Meirion is older than all of his uncles. Meirion is a capable war-leader; he was close to his grandfather Cunedda and learned much from him. Rumours abound that Meirion is favoured by the gods of war, and that they speak to him and occasionally take control of his body. He is seen as sacred by many of his warband, who are fanatically devoted to him as a living god.

MORVAN AP TYPAUN AND MORFRAN AP TYPAUN

Meirion's brothers are identical twins; their mother died while giving birth to them and Typaun cut them out of his wife's belly. Morvan has one adult son, Morfran has two, and all five are known for their erratic behaviour. Morvan and Morfran cannot be readily distinguished from each other even by their own children — even their tattoos are identical — although Meirion can somehow always tell them apart. Morfran's daughter Morfudd is betrothed to her cousin Dingad.

Morvan is an initiated apprentice to the last of Cunedda's druids; he never completed his training and yet has more skill with spirits than one might expect from an apprentice druid.

Morfran is the more bellicose of the twins; he enters battle entirely naked, his hair packed with lime to form spikes. He is able to enter a state of battle fury that makes him a fearsome foe, aided by Frenzy Root, a Votadini herb (see page 13).

BLEIDDUD AP MEIRION

Bleiddud is responsible for the administration of his father's cantref since Meirion has no interest in anything other than war. Bleiddud makes sure that farmers gather the harvest and people pay tributes; he took over this role after the death of his brother Cadwaladr in battle 8 years ago. Bleiddud remains

CLAN CEREDIG

Major Faction, Prosperous Resources, Medium Membership Size (1300 members), Devoted Dedication

Leaders
Meirion ap Typaun

Cause
To Rule Gwynedd.

Faction Skills
Ally (Gwaelod) 40%
Ally (Silures) 50%
Following 70%
Information 40%
Intrigue 35%
Subterfuge 60%

Goals
Break the alliance between Powys and the Einionydd.
Prove the superiority of the pagan faith.
Recapture Afflogion from the Irish (public).
Conquer Caer Segeint.
Convince Benlli of Rhufoniog to swap sides.
Defeat Cadwallon and Owain (public).
Force the remaining princes to accept Meirion as king (public).

 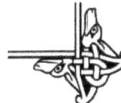

close to his father's side, and it is largely due to his efforts that Meirion's fits of madness have not become common knowledge. Bleiddud is as much a physician and a warden as he is a warrior.

The 29 year-old prince has two sons, Cynfelyn (age 5) and Cyndyn (age 3), by his brother's widow, and is also the stepfather of his 14-year-old nephew Gwrin (page 34).

EDERYN AP CUNEDDA

The Prince of Ederynion is 35 years old and the youngest of Cunedda's surviving sons. He was fostered by his nephew Meirion and his loyalty to the Ceredigydd leader is unshakeable. Ederyn has little experience in battle — he was only a child during the war — and is eager to prove himself. His mother tattooed the oak leaves of Gwynedd onto his forehead and cheeks.

DINGAD AP DYNOD

Dingad was a child when his father Dynod died 12 years ago; he is now 20 years old and has been ruling Dunodion for 7 years. Prince Dingad is betrothed to his cousin's daughter, Mordudd an Morfran. Through much of his life, Dingad has relied on the counsel of others, and yet he wants to appear decisive as befits a prince of Gwynedd. He therefore often makes foolish rulings he later regrets. For example, on the advice of a wandering druid, Dingad tried to forge a closer relationship with his estranged brother Eifion by giving him a third of his cantref; he now has misgivings regarding the benefice but has no way of taking it back.

EIFION AP DYNOD

Younger than his brother Dingad by 2 years, Eifion is without a doubt the cleverer of the two sons of Dynod. Eifion and Dingad were never friends and it was a surprise to all that, when he reached his majority (14 years old in Gwynedd), his brother made Eifion ruler of the northern part of Dunodion. Eifion has since received secret embassies from two separate parties who both want to make him the prince of all Dunodion in return for future favours. Eifion is content to allow them to come through on their promises and plans to set them against each other to avoid paying reparations.

GWAWL

The mother of Dynod, Ceredig, and Ederyn, now in her sixties. She dotes on her only living son and treats him like a child. She has a reputation as a witch: certainly those who anger her suffer terrible misfortune, but the extent (or indeed existence) of her powers are unknown (and thus at the Games Master's discretion).

ALLIES AND ENEMIES

Gwyddno of Gwaelod (page 20) is a strong supporter of the Ceredigydd. This son of Ceredig grew up not in Gwynedd, but rather in his father's own chiefdom, which he now rules himself.

Siluria (page 21) supports the Ceredigydd. Meirion has promised to set some land aside for Silures settlers; others in the faction worry that this seems remarkably cheap considering the help that King Iuchar offers and wonder what else he will demand once the war is won.

SECRETS

Typaun didn't die on Ynys Mon; he died several days later after returning completely insane. The curse of madness appears to have passed to Meirion and his brothers. Bleiddud has done his best to conceal his father's madness. He started the rumour that Meirion was god-touched to cover up the fits of erratic behaviour and fugue states; although recently, Meirion has shown signs of a descent into extreme paranoia, visual hallucinations, and fits of apoplectic rage. More worryingly, the same symptoms are showing in Meirion's brothers and nephews.

Ap Math was a druid sent by Merlin to represent his interests in Gwynedd. Morvan ap Typaun demanded he yield sacred knowledge to him. Ap Math refused, so Morvan murdered him and ate his heart, trapping his soul and stealing his powers. Morvan's brothers Morfran and Meirion are the only ones who know what he did.

FRENZY ROOT

Brought with the Votadini from Pictland, Frenzy Root is a rare herb that elite Pictish warriors chew to enhance aggression and numb pain. It takes 1d3 Minutes of chewing for the effects to take hold, during which time the warrior produces copious amounts of saliva. Frenzy Root is toxic, but the longer its user can avoid swallowing, the longer they can avoid its detrimental effects. High-ranking users sometimes spit macerated root into the mouths of their followers before battle to give them a low Potency dose.

Before the Onset Time of the poison expires, Frenzy Root temporarily adds 1, 2, or 3 Hit Points (depending on the Potency of the root) to every Hit Location. It also grants a bonus of one Difficulty Grade to all Endurance rolls and the pain of taking a Serious Wound only ever prevents a user from attacking for the minimum of 1 Turn.

All benefits are lost once the Onset Time elapses and the poison takes hold. If the loss of the extra Hit Points means the character is now suffering a Serious or Major Wound, then they automatically fail the Endurance roll to resist the wound's effects.

Application: *Ingestion*
Potency: *50%, 75%, or 100% (depending on dose)*
Resistance: *Endurance*
Onset Time: *1d6+3 Minutes*
Duration: *1d3+3 Hours*
Conditions: *Nausea strikes whether or not the character resists the poison, those who fail also suffer one, two, or three levels of Fatigue, depending on dose.*
Antidote: *Strong wine neutralises the toxin, but drinking it triggers the Nausea Condition. If the wine is successfully swallowed, the Duration of the toxin is shortened by 3 Hours*

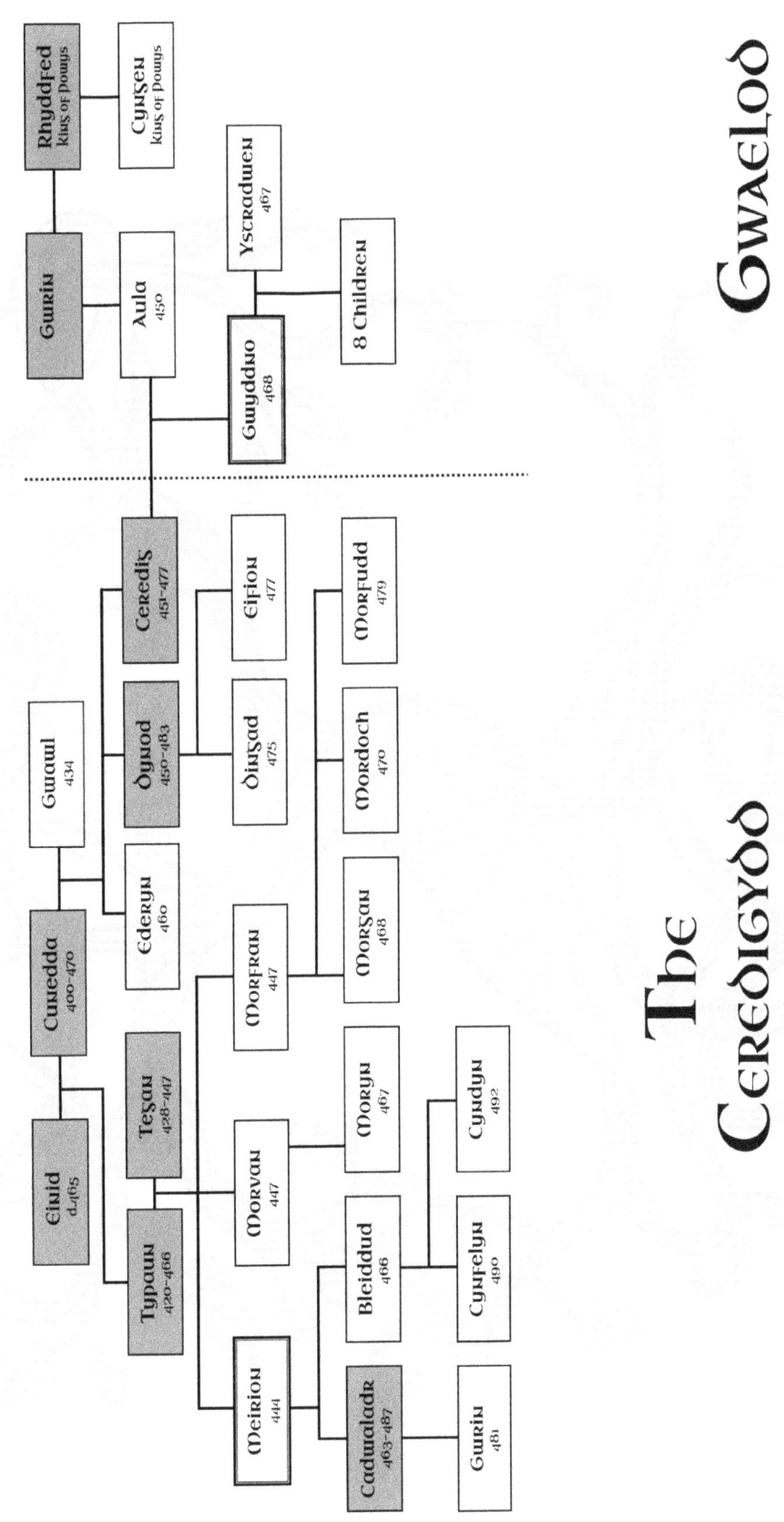

CLAN OSFAEL

Osfael, eldest of Cunedda's sons from his British queens, remained staunchly neutral in the war between his brothers, and Osfael's son Elnaw has continued this tradition. The quarrelling clans might have done more about this neutrality if Osmaeliog had been more of a prize, but it is a small and windswept island that apparently has little to offer. In truth, Osmaeliog has deep coffers filled with red gold whose provenance is a close-held secret.

Prince Elnaw is pagan but does not demand that his people follow the old gods and has even sponsored a small community of Christian monks on his island cantref. The Osmaelydd is a small clan: Elnaw and his sister are the only royals and he has just three chieftains plus Morcanwg ap Iolo, head of the bardic college at Caer Gybi, and Prior Dafyn of the monastery as his inner circle.

The island of Osmaeliog maintains a strict edict forbidding violence between Gwynedd's princes and has therefore been a neutral meeting place for the Einionydd and Ceredigydd to exchange hostages or offer concessions.

MEMBERS

ELNAW AP OSFAEL

The 29-year-old prince of Osmaeliog. He is short yet quick-witted, a skilled orator and a loremaster with bardic training. He has a prodigious memory and few know the genealogies and legends of Gwynedd better than he. Elnaw has made it his duty to settle the feud between his uncles and cousins. He has a good relationship with Cadwallon and Bleidudd, but Meirion scares him. Elnaw is yet to marry, fearing any wife he takes will threaten his precious neutrality with the political baggage that would inevitably accompany a woman of suitable status.

MORCANWG AP IOLO

The brother of Elnaw's mother and head of a small bardic college located at Caer Gybi (page 36), the only centre of learning in all Gwynedd. The bards trained here preserve the lore of the recent Pictish royals as well as that of those who came before. Morcanwg takes a hefty dose of poetic license with his knowledge and is always able to "remember" (i.e., invent) an obscure piece of lore that suits his agenda. However, he has his nephew's best interests at heart.

PRIOR DAFYN

A native of Gwynedd who trained as a priest in Powys and now heads a community of eight monks in Osmaeliog. Dafyn is suspicious of Eledenius (page 22); he sees ambition and pride in the man and does not consider these to be saintly qualities. Dafyn is quietly spoken and carefully considers his words before opening his mouth.

ALLIES AND ENEMIES

Much like his father before him, Elnaw has been careful to maintain equal relations with both the Einionydd and the Ceredigydd. He was also host to Merlin's druid Ap Math before he disappeared.

Elnaw's sorest enemy is the Blackshield Irish (page 21), who have ravaged the southern and western coast of his cantref. He has placed a bounty on Connor mac Eird, equal to a plate of gold the size of the Irishman's head and as thick as a goose's eggshell; he offers the same in silver for Flann Ainsheasccar or any of the captains of the Irish ships.

CLAS OSFAEL

Major Faction, Prosperous Resources, Small Membership Size (70 members), Moderate Dedication

Leaders
Elnaw ap Osfael

Cause
End the Civil War.

Faction Skills
Ally (Einionydd) 30%
Ally (Ceredygidd) 30%
Following 20%
Information 50%
Intrigue 40%
Subterfuge 25%

Goals
Destroy the Blackshield Irish (public).
Negotiate a truce between the Ceredygdd and Einionydd (public).
Secure and maintain a stable role for Osmaeliog (public).
Elect a new King of Gwynedd (public).

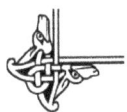 

SECRETS

The wealth of Osmaeliog derives from a cache of coins found beneath Caer Gybi, left by fleeing Romans. If any of the gold is brought too close to Ynys Mon, it is possible for a Roman ghost to "ride" the gold and temporarily escape the prison of the island (page 43). Several have been paroled in this way; most are angry at the pagan Britons and seek revenge against them before they are drawn inexorably back to Ynys Mon.

The Venedoti

The Cynwy valley in Arfon cantref is home to the last remaining members of the Lleyn and Rhos royal families, scions of the Gangani and Deceangi tribes who once ruled in Gwynedd. Their existence here is a secret: all the locals are loyal to the cause or else pretend loyalty to preserve their lives. The leader of the Venedoti is Maeldaf whose father Dylan was, at the time of Cunedda's invasion, the crown prince of Lleyn and Rhos.

The Venedoti plot against the Ceredigydd and the Einionydd in secret. The Einionydd are their particular targets since they occupy the Venedoti heartlands. They perceive Dogfeil to be the weakest prince and therefore their first target; Afallach (page 22) has plans for Benlli that will leave Rhufuniog free for the taking. They will then move against the sons of Einion. The Ceredigydd for the most part do not occupy Venedoti lands, but the Pictish line of Typaun is anathema to Maeldaf, since Typaun helped Cunedda slaughter his family. If Meirion and his brothers were somehow eliminated, then Maeldaf could tolerate Ederyn as the leader of the Ceredigydd; his Venedoti mother redeems him. Maeldaf could also make peace with Osfael (who is Maeldaf's cousin through the maternal line) and the sons of Dynod (who are of Gangani blood), as long as they make no claim over Venedoti lands.

The Venedoti are too small to be able to achieve their ambitious objectives. Their best chance is to provoke open warfare between the Ceredigydd and Einionydd, and take advantage of the turmoil to strike when their foes are weakened. If Afallach is successful in his plotting, they will gain powerful supernatural help that will undoubtedly improve their chances of winning.

Members

Only native Britons descended from Eudaf Hen, the ancestor of both the Gangani and Deceangi, can become members of the Venedoti. Membership is secret, most are farmers and churls, and they can be found throughout Gwynedd, often working directly for chieftains of the Ceredigydd or Einionydd.

Maeldaf ap Dylan

Maeldaf considers himself to be King of Lleyn, dispossessed of his homeland by the sons of Einion. He lives right under their noses in Cynwy, close to the ancient capital of the kingdom. Maeldaf has seen 58 summers and can remember the time before Cunedda and his Picts.

Dylan Traws ap Tudwal

Dylan was crown prince of the Venedoti when the Picts came. He witnessed Cunedda execute his father Tudwal and brother Cynfawr, and rape his sister Olwen. Now fast approaching his ninth decade, Dylan is twisted and hate-filled, and yearns for the day he can assume his rightful place as the King of Rhos.

Meddyf an Maeldaf

On her eighteenth birthday, this daughter of Maeldaf took a secret blood-oath to end the life of Cadwallon ap Einion, a man she then married later the same day. None of her new family knows her true descent or political affiliation. Her mission is to remain hidden and remain close to Cadwallon, feed information back to the Venedoti, and prepare to kill her husband as soon as Owain is dealt with. She has now been undercover as a spy and assassin for 10 years and she has disobeyed her family just once: she allowed her pregnancies to come to full term, arguing that if she didn't give Cadwallon children he would set her aside for a more fertile wife.

VENEDOTI

Major Faction, Poor Resources, Small Membership Size (50 members), Zealous Dedication

Leaders
Maeldaf ap Dylan

Cause
To Rule Gwynedd.

Faction Skills
Ally - None
Following 30%
Information 65%
Intrigue 35%
Subterfuge 75%

Goals
Install Eifion as Prince of Dunodion.
Defeat or kill Dogfeil.
Form alliance with Elnaw.
Kill Meirion.
Kill Owain and install Dylan as the King of Rhos (Rhos, Rhufoniog, and Dogfeilion cantrefs).
Kill Cadwallon and install Maeldaf as the King of Lleyn (Arfon, Afflogion, and Dunodion cantrefs).

ALLIES AND ENEMIES

The Venedoti have no allies — there is no one they can trust with their secrets.

They consider all invaders, whether Picts, Irish, or Ordovices, to be enemies; although since none of the other factions are currently aware of them, they have no enemies actively working against them.

SECRETS

Meddyf still professes her loyalty to the blood-oath to her family she made on her wedding day, but secretly she has fallen in love with Cadwallon and does nothing to jeopardise her son Maelgwyn. She secretly hopes her family will see Maelgwyn as an acceptable Venedoti king.

Cywyrd (Mythic Britain, page 222), father of Guinevere and Gwenhwyfach, is the brother of Cendal. He takes no part in his family's conspiracy other than to proclaim to all who will hear him that he and his daughters are the last of the Deceangi in an attempt to hide the family's existence. If Arthur both marries Guinevere and becomes High King, Maeldaf is not above using blackmail to secure favours from his well-placed kinswoman.

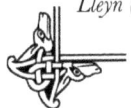 

CENDAL AP CYNFAWR

Cendal is Maeldaf's cousin and the son of the last King of Rhos. He was only four when Cunedda executed his father. He was brought up in fosterage, but told of his true heritage when he came of age and has been loyal to the Venedoti cause ever since. Maeldaf and Dylan have chosen him as their crown prince. Now in his early fifties, he was foster-father to Benlli ap Rhwfon and indoctrinated the impressionable young prince into the belief that he is destined to be King of Gwynedd.

MYTHIC BRITAIN: GWYNEDD

The Venedoti

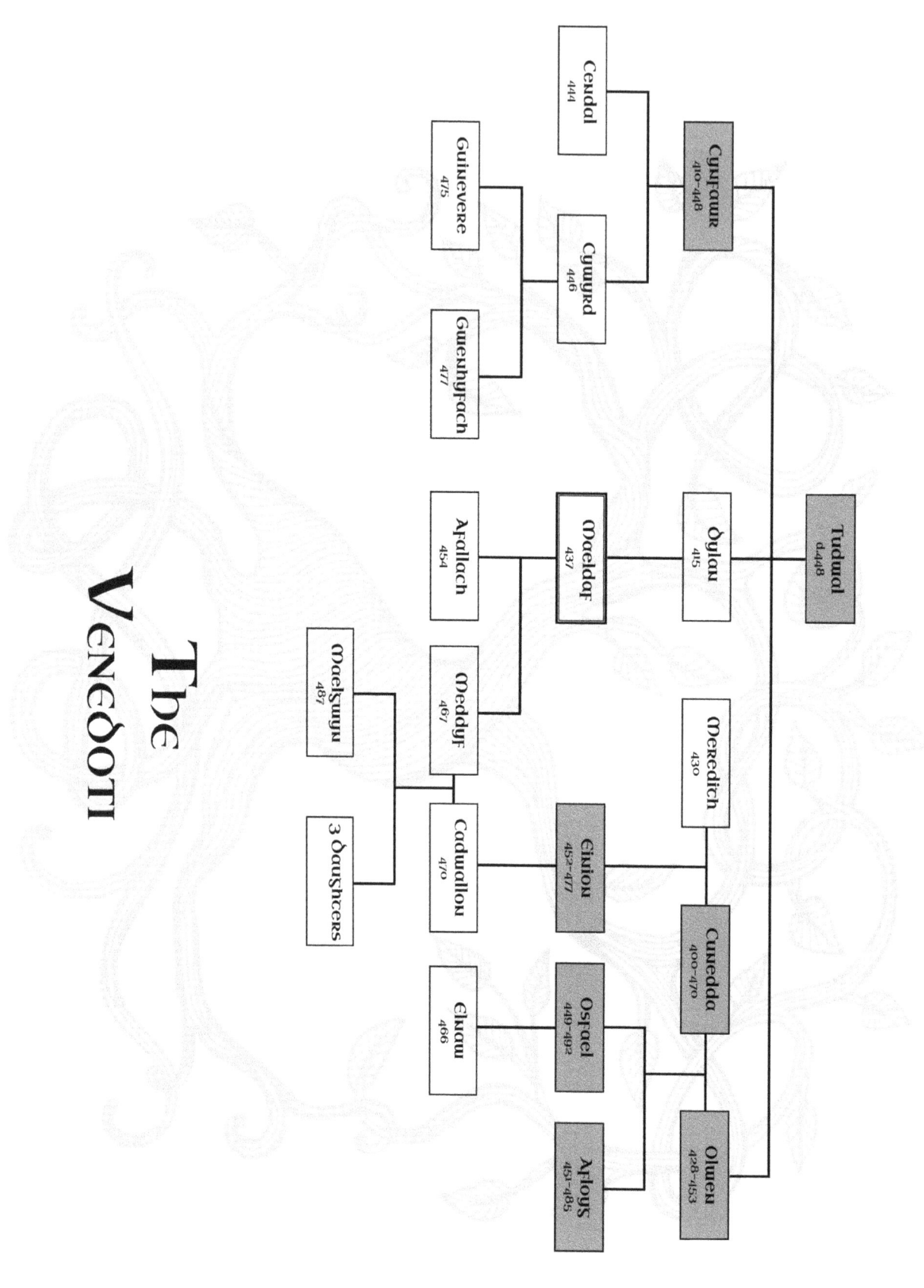

Other Factions

In addition to the native Gwynedd factions, there are several other parties interested in the contest for the country's crown. In the case of Powys and Siluria, the faction statistics are for those dedicated to the cause of Gwynedd and do not reflect the power of these kingdoms as a whole.

Gwaelod

Minor Faction, Prosperous Resources, Tiny Membership Size (15 members), Moderate Dedication

Leaders
Gwyddno ap Ceredig

Cause
Receive Ceredig's Birthright.

Faction Skills
Ally (Powys) 40%
Following 20%
Information 40%
Intrigue 45%
Subterfuge 20%

Gwaelod is a province of Powys that borders Meirionydd. Its chief is Gwyddno, son of Ceredig ap Cunedda and Aula, a Powysian princess. Gwaelod originally belonged to Aula's father Gwrin Farfdrwch, who was the younger brother of King Rhyddfedd of Powys. When the province was overcome by the Irish, Cunedda gave Aula shelter in Gwynedd where she met and married Ceredig. Cunedda did not believe her when she accused her brother-in-law Einion of raping her, which precipitated the rebellion and exile of Ceredig and Aula from Gwynedd. Ceredig swore an oath to his wife's cousin King Cyngen, and drove the Irish out of Gwaelod and retook it in his new king's name.

Gwyddno is caught in an awkward position. A faction fights for control of Gwynedd in his father's name, but even if the Ceredigydd win, he'll get no benefit from it. Relations are cool between Gwyddno, a Christian Briton, and his cousin Meirion, a pagan Pict; yet, Aula has instilled in her son a deep hatred for Einion and his kin and he cannot bring himself to support them either. Cyngen has given Gwyddno freedom to pursue his goal for his birthright in Gwynedd, but does not brook any direct interference in Powys's plans.

Gwyddno is married to Ystradwen and has a daughter Mererid and sons Idris, Rhun, Dyfnwal, Eifionydd, Elffin, Sandde, and Edern.

Goals
Be recognised as a candidate for Gwynedd's crown.
Take control of the Ceredigydd from the sons of Typaun.

Powys

Minor Faction, Average Resources, Small Membership Size (70 members), Casual Dedication

Leaders
King Cyngen

Cause
Get a Christian as king of Gwynedd.

Faction Skills
Ally (Gwyddno) 20%
Following 20%

Information 25%
Intrigue 50%
Subterfuge 35%

Cyngen's father Rhyddfedd pledged support to Einion and his followers as recent converts to Christianity, and the current King of Powys has continued this alliance. Cyngen keeps a permanent force of spearmen deployed on Gwynedd's eastern border, ostensibly to guard against Cornovian aggression from Caer Ffrydd. However, these men have orders to support military actions against Einion's clan that can be easily explained later as acting in the defence of Powys and the Ordovices. Cyngen privately supports Gwyddno's support of the Ceredigydd, although he publicly pretends to ignore it. Gwyddno is his backup plan — even if the Ceredigydd win despite Cyngen's best efforts, then Powys can still influence its northern neighbour through his vassal.

Powys secretly wants control over Ynys Mon (page 43). Cyngen believes he can destroy British druidry by sanctifying the island in the name of Christ. He has no particular hatred for pagans, but believes that to complete his mission to unify Western Britain, he must unite everyone under a common religion.

Madoc, the brother of Cunedda's third wife Meredith, is the main contact between Powys and the Einionydd. He rules the fortress of Dinas Bran on Gwynedd's eastern border.

GOALS

Support Cadwallon against the Ceredigydd.
Support Owain to become independent of his brother.
Neutralise Benlli.
Support Dogfeil's attempt on the throne.

SILURIA

Minor Faction, Poor Resources, Small Membership Size (50 members), Moderate Dedication

LEADERS
King Iuchar

CAUSE
Settle the Deisi Irish.

FACTION SKILLS
Ally (Deisi Irish) 45%
Following 40%
Information 20%
Intrigue 20%
Subterfuge 20%

King Iuchar supports Ceredig's clan, although has little interest in who ends up ruling Gwynedd. He would prefer to see a pagan wearing the Oaken Torc, and cannot deny that an ally in the north would be useful in his plans to conquer Gwent and ultimately Powys. His main reason for supporting Ceredig's clan is to make good on his promise to his Deisi Muman Irish allies (blood-enemies of the Blackshield Irish) and find lands in which they can settle.

GOALS
Kill Connor mac Eird (public).
Support Meirion's bid for Gwynedd's crown.
Secure lands for the Deisi Irish in return for supporting Meirion.

BLACKSHIELD IRISH

Minor Faction, Average Resources, Medium Membership Size (220 members), Devoted Dedication

LEADERS
Connor mac Eird

CAUSE
Establish a kingdom in Afflogion.

FACTION SKILLS
No Allies
Following 50%
Information 50%
Intrigue 30%
Subterfuge 40%

Irish settlers from the Province of Laigin were one of the scavengers who picked over the bones of Gwynedd before the coming of Cunedda. The Pictish warlord drove them out, but following his death, they have slunk back and now maintain a substantial presence in the cantref of Afflogion. The Blackshield Irish haunt the seas of Tremadog Bay, preventing all travel by sea. Their leader is Connor mac Eird, a Laigin prince and pirate, and his second-in-command is Flann Ainsheasccar (Flann the Restless). Connor accepted exile after a kinsman became king; it was either that or accept a mutilation that would disqualify him from becoming king himself one day (Irish kings are required to be without physical flaw).

Connor's clan, the Eóganachta, are blood-enemies of the Deisi Muman, who fled Ireland to escape the feud and settled mostly in Siluria. The Blackshield Irish consider the Silures their enemy for offering shelter to the Deisi and have no love for their allies the Ceredigydd. They are also arrayed against the Einionydd, since the land they occupy by rights belongs to

Cadwallon ap Einion. Connor considers the Head of Bran (page 47) to be a relic of his clan; he is a descendant of Matholwch who captured Bran and took possession of his body. The Head was stolen by Britons and brought back to Gwynedd, and one of Connor's goals in coming here was to retrieve it and use its prophetic powers to guide his hand.

GOALS
Control the seaways of Gwynedd.
Possess the Head of Bran.
Secure lasting truce with the ruler of Gwynedd.

DRUIDS AND PRIESTS

The following individuals are active in Gwynedd, but they pursue their own agendas alone rather than act as part of a faction. Notably, Merlin has no representation in Gwynedd; previously a druid trained by Askrigg named Ap Math was his agent here, but he has recently disappeared (page 13).

AFALLACH AP MAELDAF
The eldest son of Maeldaf of the Venedoti, Afallach is in his early forties. He is tall with long raven-dark hair, but suffers from a congenital defect resulting in shortened arms and just two fingers and a thumb on each hand. Trained by the last surviving druid of the Gangani, Afallach styles himself the "High Druid of Gwynedd," but that position has not existed for centuries and he has not sought recognition from the other High Druids. One of his most powerful spirits is the vengeful wraith of his aunt Olwen, who was Cunedda's queen. He lives on Ynys Lannog.

Afallach is a member of the Venedoti faction, but supports them in the way only druids can. He has convinced Prince Benlli of Rhufoniog that he is the rightful king of the united Gwynedd. Afallach is planning that Benlli's reign will last one day before Afallach sacrifices him to the gods; Benlli's royal blood will be used to wash Ynys Mon clean, banishing its curse (page 43). Once it is clean, Afallach plans to recruit the ghosts of his druid ancestors to the Venedoti cause in opposing the Pictish usurpers.

EITHNE OF THE EVIL EYE
Eithne was trained by Tadgh, High Druid of the Silures. She is a tall woman of arrogant demeanour and keeps her left eye perpetually closed — beneath the lid is a baleful spirit of great power, whose gaze can cause madness and death.

Eithne is an occasional visitor to Meirion's court at Caer Aderyn and provides spiritual support for the Ceredigydd. Like most Silures, Eithne is a devotee of Crom Cruach and demands regular sacrifices to keep her god well-fed. Many of these sacrifices are Blackshield Irish captives taken in raids.

SAINT ELEDENIUS
Born Elidan, son of Prince Dogfeil, this Christian priest now goes by his baptismal name Eledenius. Bishop Frych of Powys has promised he will become the first bishop of a united Gwynedd. Despite his young age (he is only 22 years old), he has already proved to be a man of great holiness and several miracles are attributed to him. His ambition may prove his downfall; he seems to believe that his destiny protects him, but political machinations have no regard for sanctity.

PLACES

This chapter details the major locations in Gwynedd, and likely encounters when travelling through or around the area. Refer to the maps on pages 52 and 53 for more information.

AFFLOGION

The cantref of Afloyg, son of Cunedda and Olwen. Afloyg never married and had no acknowledged children; he named Cadwallon ap Einion as his heir and died a decade ago after a long illness. However, the neglected cantref fell to Irish raids, and the capital of Boduan is now occupied by Connor mac Eird and numerous Irish settlements have sprung up around the coast that support the Blackshield fleet moored at Aberdaron.

Unlike the other eight cantrefs, Afflogion has no mountains; rather, it has a central spine of hills surrounded by coastal plains. The southern side of these hills is sheltered by Tremadog Bay and has rich farmlands, all claimed by the Blackshield Irish. The northern plain is exposed to the storm-prone sea and is mostly deserted.

ARFON

One of the two cantrefs given to Einion, son of Cunedda and Meredith, and now ruled by his son Cadwallon. Arfon's royal seat is Caer Segeint (Segontium to the Romans), which was Cunedda's capital as well. Arfon's second major hillfort is Canovium (or Caer Rhun), which is ruled by Deithlyn, Cadwallon's maternal grandfather.

Arfon is dominated by the Eryri Mountains, which have the highest peaks in the region, with Mount Erith (page 25) being the highest.

DOGFEILION

The cantref of Dogfeil, son of Cunedda and Meredith. Dogfeil still rules here, the eldest of Cunedda's two remaining sons. A large portion of the kingdom is occupied by Gwernfor, the Great Marsh. Dogfeil's fortress of Rhuthun lies in the middle of Gwernfor.

DUNODION

The cantref of Dynod, son of Cunedda and Gwawl; Dynod's son Dingad is the current prince. The capital of Ardudwy was built by Lleu Llaw Gyffes (known as the god Lugh elsewhere in Britain), who was a vassal of High King Math in the Time of Heroes.

The land to the north of the River Dwyryd is called Eifionydd and belongs to the prince's younger brother Eifion, who rules from the hillfort of Dolbenmaen.

The sacred site of Bryn Cader Faner (Magical Strength 50%) is a round cairn surrounded by 30 thin pillars jutting upwards and outwards from the cairn as if they have exploded out of the earth.

EDERYNION

The cantref of Ederyn, son of Cunedda and Gwawl, who is still its prince. Ederyn is a keen hunter, and he often stalks the deer in the valleys of his mountainous homeland with his sons. He is a devotee of the hunting god Cunomaglos and forbids the trapping or killing of wolves within his cantref. His Roman-built fort of Caer Gai was constructed on an outcrop overlooking the river leading to the sacred site of Llyn Tegid (Magical Strength 75%). Llyn Tegid is known for its crystal-clear waters, its mirror-like surface, and its shrines to the four gods honoured here: Tegid Voel, a giant water god; his wife Ceridwen, the Crooked Goddess; and their children Afagddu the Hideous and Creirwy the Beautiful. It is said that the gods confer blessings to those who make appropriate sacrifices at their shrines.

Meirionydd

The cantref of Meirion ap Typaun, the grandson of Cunedda and his Pictish wife Einid. Meirion may rule the cantref that bears his name, but his son Bleiddud shoulders most of the work. Caer Aderyn, the "Fort of the Birds," is named after the large number of carrion birds that wheel in the sky around the peak, attracted by the corpses of bandits and thieves with which Meirion decorates his fortress.

Osmaeliog

The cantref of Osfael, son of Cunedda and Olwen. Osfael's son Elnaw is now the prince here. Osmaeliog is the smallest and most remote of Gwynedd's nine cantrefs, consisting of a small island lying off the west coast of Ynys Mon. Elnaw's capital is Caer Gybi, a small three-walled Roman fort and its only fortified town. Caer Gybi is home to a small bardic college (page 15), the only lore centre in Gwynedd.

Rhos

One of the two cantrefs given to Einion, son of Cunedda and Meredith. Owain ap Einion rules Rhos from Din Arth ("Fort Bear"). It was one of the main settlements of the Venedoti and has a massive, well-built wall made of quarried stone.

Rhufoniog

The mountainous cantref of Rhwfon, son of Cunedda and Meredith. Benlli ap Rhwfon is now prince of Rhufoniog. Caer Dathyl, also called "the fortress of enchantment," was built by the druid-kings Math and Mathonwy who once ruled Gwynedd in the Time of Heroes, and it is a sacred site (Magical Strength 25%).

Gwaelod

Not part of Gwynedd but beholden to Powys. About half of Gwaelod's land area has been reclaimed from the sea to the west of Gwynedd, an area called the Maes Gwyddno ("Plain of Gwyddno"), behind a wall that holds back the sea. Three massive earthworks called sarnau support the wall; the longest is Sarn Fawr in the north, which extends nearly 20 kilometres from shore; then there is the short Sarn y Bwch; and finally Sarn Gynfelyn, which terminates in Caer Wyddno, home to Gwaelod's chief Gwyddno ap Ceredig. This area encloses 16 settlements that take advantage of the rich alluvial mud from the rivers to grow crops and raise sheep on the salt marshes, but these activities are secondary to the gold that the inhabitants of Gwaelod extract from the mud and refine for their lord. The other main settlement of Gwaelod is Caer Rihog on Sarn Fawr.

Ynys Mon

One of the principal sacred sites in Britain, Ynys Mon has been off-limits for over four centuries following the massacre of the druids. Connor mac Eird has claimed possession of the island in the name of the Blackshield Irish, but his men have done nothing more than stand in the surf and thrown spears ashore to stake their claim.

Ynys Mon is protected by the powers unleashed by the druids at the moment of their death, fuelled by their own life's blood. A score of druids sacrificed themselves in the name of revenge, and it is said that Abandinus the god of bloodshed and Agrona the goddess of carnage walked the earth in physical form on that day. The souls of an entire generation of druids and those of countless Romans are trapped on the island, forever barred from the Afterlife.

The sacred site known as Bryn Celli Ddu (Magical Strength 100%) is one of the key focal points of the druidic religion. It is a mound of earth 26 metres in diameter contained within kerb stones. There is a trilithon marking the entrance to the passage within, which is 9 metres long and lined with vertical slabs of stone. The chamber at the end of the passage contains a smooth stone pillar, and on the back wall, there is a stone covered in sinuous serpentine carvings that wind around both sides. The chamber is known as the Eye of the Great Red Dragon and is believed to be a window into the Spirit World, allowing direct communication between human and spirit. Anyone climbing into the well is discorporated and their soul sent to the World of Spirits.

More information on Ynys Mon can be found on page 43.

Dinas Affaraon

In the Eryri Mountains, the holy Mount Erith looms over the border between Arfon and Dunodion. Vortigern built the fortress of Dinas Emrys on its slopes (on a site sacred to the Old People), and it was here that Merlin gave the High King the Prophecy of the Two Dragons (Mythic Britain, page 9). The hillfort was soon abandoned by Vortigern, and Merlin claimed it as his. Now called Dinas Affaraon, it belongs to no king or people but to Britain as a whole. No one visits Dinas Affaraon except for Brythonic druids, who sometimes complete their training here. On rare occasions, there might be more than one apprentice-teacher pair in residence. The site is guarded by two giants, Aradr Gawr and Rhita Gawr, mortal enemies yet united in their purpose to protect the next generation of British druids.

ENCOUNTERS

Random encounters in Gwynedd mostly take place in the mountains. The coastal region and the valleys are generally inhabited, and encounters tend to be with farmers and shepherds.

Most encounters are with native inhabitants of the mountains who use the natural terrain to their own advantage. The mountains are treacherous with rockslides and hanging boulders, riddled with natural caves and blind-ending cwms, and strewn with bottomless pools of dark water and flood-prone streams. The broken terrain provides numerous opportunities for ambushes, treacherous footing, and sudden sinkholes. Snow and ice are a hazard for at least half the year, and sudden fogs, howling winds, and driving hail can occur year-round.

d100	Encounter	Description
01–07	Travellers	Foreigners (most likely Silures or Ordovices) on the same route as the characters. They may be a diplomatic mission or traders.
08–15	Adventurers	They could be following rumours of a dragon, serving as mercenaries travelling to a new employer, or tracking down a wrongdoer.
16–25	Shepherds	If more than one, then they are all children. Accompanied by a flock of 3d8 sheep or goats, and perhaps a dog.
26–40	Hare coursers	2d3–1 hunters, each with a swift-looking dog. They may have been lucky and are carrying a brace of hares.
41–50	Raiders	1d3+3 warriors from an opposing faction. They do their best to remain unseen, but are unlikely to ambush a group of adventurers since they probably have a specific mission.
51–52	Hermit	Found alone, while gathering berries and mushrooms. Probably has a reason for wanting to be left alone: often religious (equal chance of Christian or Pagan), but may also be in self-imposed exile, in hiding, or simply mad.
53–60	Patrol	1d3+3 warriors from a local faction. They may have been warned against interlopers and might mistake the characters for their target.
61–66	Deer	A red buck. Stats as a horse (Mythras, page 251) but add Antlers (Size H, Reach M, Damage 1d10). Alternatively, a herd of 3d6 hinds and young.
67–72	Wild goats	1d8+4 shaggy creatures with impressive horns. They have kids and aggressively defend them.
73–77	Bear	Mythras, page 230. Typically alone, might be a mother with 1d3 cubs.
78–81	Wolves	Mythras, page 272. A pack of 2d4–1 individuals.
82–85	Giant weasel	Use the statistics of a lion (Mythras, page 253) but with Stealth 70% and the Grappler and Leaper Abilities. The characters might interrupt its meal (a horse) or be stalked by the creature as it hunts.
86–88	Gwyll	A *gwyll* (pl. *gwyllion*) is a nature (goat) spirit. They can Manifest in the shape of a goat and have Dominion of goats as well. They are mischievous, sometimes wicked, and love to waylay and mislead travellers.
89–91	Hairy Man	The Hairy Men (*gwyr blewog*; sg. *gwr blewog*) are a non-human race that predates the Britons. They are shorter than humans and do not use clothes, relying on their long tresses of red hair and (for the males) beards to keep them warm. They prefer to keep away from travellers, but grow unaccountably enraged by certain actions such as whistling. Use the statistics for baboons (Mythras, page 227) but with INT rather than INS. A particularly unpleasant member of the race is Canthrig Bwt, a child-eating witch who haunts the slopes of Mount Erith.
92–94	Ceffyl Dwr	A magical and malicious horse found near mountain pools and waterfalls. They have fiery eyes and a black coat, but can shapechange into ordinary ponies or mist. They can fly and radiate a dark, foreboding presence. They are known to entice a rider to mount and then fly over a lake before turning into mist. Use the statistics of a horse (Mythras, page 251) but add the Flying and Intimidate Abilities.
95–97	Afanc	A monstrous beaver that dwells in high lakes. It is highly territorial, but only a threat to those who venture onto the water. Afanc can create whirlpools that can capsize boats and drown swimmers. Use the statistics of a boar (Mythras, page 231) but with the Swimmer Ability and the Tailed Quadruped Hit Locations.
98–00	Giant	Giants (cewri, sg. gawr) are not uncommon in Gwynedd. There are two tribes: those loyal to Rhita Gawr who are hostile to humans and those sworn to Aradr Gawr who prefer to leave humans alone (Mythras, page 245).

QUARRELLING PRINCES

Arthur is keen to settle the conflict between the Ceredigydd and the Einionydd so that the ruler of a united Gwynedd can lend its strength to the Alliance of Britain. He asks the characters to accompany two diplomats into Gwynedd to start the peace process. Note Arthur's initial approach to the situation in Gwynedd is quite naïve; like the rest of Britain, he is ignorant of how entrenched the two factions are. The purpose of this adventure is to introduce the characters to the politics of Gwynedd so they can realise the magnitude of any reconciliation attempts.

Some of the scenes and events described herein are dependent on the actions of the characters earlier in the adventure. There are also several scenes and follow-on stories that have been left for the Games Master to develop. Make sure to read the adventure fully first before deciding which ones to develop.

ARTHUR'S NEGOTIATORS

The two negotiators are Felimid and Moccus. Felimid is a Dumnonian bard trained in Lindinis, who takes the lead when speaking with the Ceredigydd. Moccus is a monk from Eboracum, recommended by Queen Elliw; he is chief envoy amongst the Einionydd. The two have orders to work with one another, despite the changing leadership roles, to demonstrate that pagans and Christians can work together.

The Games Master might plan a short prelude where the characters bring the two negotiators together. They might need to extract Felimid from a bawdyhouse in Lindinis, perhaps dealing with his gambling creditors. Alternatively, Moccus might be sequestered in a monastery at Eboracum and must be convinced that the queen herself has assigned him this task. If the adventuring group is predominantly Christian, then it might be worth setting them the first of these tasks and directing a pagan-dominant group to the second. This reversal gives the characters an opportunity to forge a connection with the negotiator towards whom they are less inclined.

Once together, Felimid and Moccus can brief the characters on the situation in Gwynedd; however, their knowledge is assembled from travellers' accounts and is neither complete nor accurate. They agree that Meirionydd and Ederynion are part of the Ceredigydd and that Arfon, Afflogion, and Rhos are Einionydd, but have conflicting accounts regarding the affiliations of the other cantrefs. Felimid's sources say that Osmaeliog is no more, whereas Moccus's accounts say it controls all of Ynys Mon and is the strongest of them all. The two counsellors also argue over the qualifying conditions for becoming king of Gwynedd: Moccus has a book of Gwynedd law codes but it dates from before Cunedda and Felimid has memorised Votadini edicts but admits that he doesn't know whether Cunedda used them or replaced them with something else.

Felimid and Moccus can be run as Non-Player Characters or as either second characters for the players (perhaps those with characters who have few social skills) or controlled communally. Any Standard Skill not mentioned in their descriptions is at its base value.

FELIMID THE BARD

A short, slight man, with a quick smile and friendly eyes. He prefers to go beardless, which gives him a boyish charm, although he wears full sideburns to advertise his maturity. Felimid typically wears a green cape over red braecci and a white tunic covered with intricate interwoven embroidery. He has tattoos of sunwheels on the backs of both hands. He is never far from his harp, which he carries in a waterproof case. When necessary, he carries a willow branch stripped of its bark, which announces his status as a bard and envoy.

Moccus the Monk

A bulky man with a large nose. His clumsiness has become a joke amongst his fellow monks. He has a monastic tonsure and no facial hair, and wears a pale brown habit and darker cloak, both of which are often travel-stained. He carries a leather satchel with a psalter, stylus, wax tablet, and other essentials. Moccus is sharp-witted, and while pious, he does not flaunt his faith or evangelise to pagans.

SETTING OUT

The characters should plan the route into Gwynedd and decide on the agenda for the trip. Caer Segeint and Caer Aderyn should be on the list, since these are the homes of the faction leaders, but the characters may also want to meet with some of the other princes. To allow time to prepare events in locations other than the four detailed in the following sections, the Games Master should ask the characters to determine where they'd like to go and to whom they'd like to talk.

The characters should also discuss — with the Games Master providing input as Felimid and Moccus — what they hope to achieve. The decades-long blood feud cannot be solved overnight, but Arthur wants to understand the conflict between the two sides and perhaps hear some terms of peace that each faction considers acceptable.

The journey to Gwynedd should give the characters opportunities to get to know Felimid and Moccus. The negotiators are tolerant of each other's faith, but have many other reasons to disagree. To contrast their viewpoints, the Games Master can design one or more events targeted specifically at one or other of these new companions. Here are two possible examples:

- The adult child of a farmer who has offered the characters hospitality is particularly fetching and seems to be flirting with Felimid. Felimid might be tempted to dally, but the prudish Moccus would strongly disapprove. However, if the monk guards the young person's virtue too closely, Moccus may be suspected of having his own prurient interests in the young person's chastity.

- A person is accused of commanding devils to curse their Christian neighbour. Felimid is likely to automatically defend a pagan over a Christian, whereas for Moccus, finding the truth and preventing an injustice are more important than religious affiliation.

ENTERING GWYNEDD

Getting to Gwynedd offers the Games Master opportunities to include additional scenes depending on the route taken. These are optional but allow the characters to meet the Manx Traders (see below) and combine forces with them against adversity.

If the characters approach Gwynedd from the south, they discover that the chief of Caer Sws is preventing anyone heading north into Ceredigydd lands and he is not prepared to disobey these orders without a direct command from the King of Powys. This could take weeks and the characters might prefer to sneak into Gwynedd, avoiding the Powysian patrols.

The characters may instead choose to travel to Gwynedd from Middle Britain. They almost certainly travel via Caer Ffridd in Cornovia (Mythic Britain, page 34) and might easily get on the wrong side of Chief Llwyld's paranoia. For example, one of the important Cornovian families who is eager to ingratiate itself with Arthur might offer hospitality the characters, but their hosts are Vortigern-loyalists and thus enemies of Llwyld.

If the characters sail to Gwynedd, they face dangers on the sea. Siluria would prefer no outside interference in Gwynedd and might seek to stop any ships entering their coastal waters. When the characters get closer to Gwynedd, the Blackshield Irish are a certain threat; they oppose any boats in Tremadog Bay or between the Lleyn Peninsula and Osmaeliog (see " Dangerous Waters," page 36, for more details).

The Manx Traders

During the journey to Gwynedd, the characters are assisted by two traders by the names of Saoirse and Tiorrach. This pair is also heading for Gwynedd, and think it sensible to combine forces with the characters and pool resources. How this help manifests depends very much on the characters' entry route: they might help the characters sneak out of Caer Sws, or vouch for the characters before Llwyld. Saoirse and Tiorrach claim to be from the Isle of Man, but a successful Goidelic Language roll reveals that their accent is not Manx but actually from the south of Ireland — they are Blackshield Irish and spies for Connor mac Eird.

Claiming to have no specific agenda, the traders propose they continue to travel with the characters, in the interests of safety. They claim to be interested in setting up trade opportunities with anyone who can enrich their king, but in particular the Einionydd are their targets. If necessary, they offer a share of the first year's profits in return for the

characters' help — they can afford to be surprisingly generous with this promise as they do not intend to honour it, but are negotiating for the sake of keeping up the pretence.

The Einionydd Council

Approaching Einion's clan involves travel to Caer Segeint in the heart of Gwynedd. There are several Roman-built roads (in various states of repair) that lead through the mountain valleys; Caer Segeint is accessible from the southwest (via Dunodion) or from the northeast. The Games Master can challenge the characters with one or more encounters during their journey through the mountains, chosen from or rolled on the Gwynedd Mountain Encounters table (page 26).

Upon arriving at Caer Segeint, Cadwallon is a gracious and generous host. However, he does not meet formally with the embassy from Arthur until the full council of the four princes of the Einionydd (himself, Owain, Benlli, and Dogfeil) can gather. A successful Lore (politics) or Hard Insight roll suggests this is a sign of the weakness of the Einionydd; Cadwallon is clearly unwilling or unable to exercise his leadership, constrained by his kin.

The Council Gathers

While they wait, Cadwallon provides entertainment in the form of a feast, a contest of games (see pages 31-32), and an *eisteddfod* (a poetry competition). The characters have an opportunity to practise their skills and perhaps show off a little. (Some traditional Celtic games are described on page 32.) Owain arrives on the second day, Mor ap Rhufion (standing in for Prince Benlli) on the fourth, and finally Dogfeil on the fifth.

The characters may find Owain a refreshing change from the aloof Cadwallon. The younger brother is fond of a party and throws himself into the contests with gusto. He opens his brother's cellars and initiates drinking games, hitherto absent from the contests. Owain is competitive (and skilled at it), but is magnanimous in defeat and presents valuable prizes from his own coffers to the winners. If any of the characters have an interest in hunting, Owain knows where to find some boar, which would be a welcome addition to the feast.

The last day of the feast all the princes are in attendance and it is a more solemn affair. Eledenius (who accompanied his father here) leads prayers, as well as formal dancing, music, and scriptural recitation. Eledenius asks Moccus several pointed questions across the hall; it is clear that he is testing the monk's credentials in doctrine and church lore. There is an accusatory tone; it is clear to everyone that this is no idle banter. The Games Master should conduct the interrogation as a Social Conflict (Mythras Companion, page 14); or, if those rules are not available, as a series of Opposed Rolls against suitable skills (Influence, Lore (Christian), Oratory, and the like). How Moccus survives this intellectual battle decides the tenor of the morrow's negotiations.

The characters are not expected to contribute to the council meeting; they do not even need to attend if they would rather not. If the characters choose not attend the council, they are free to explore Caer Segeint and the docks. They may wish to visit Cunedda's tomb and see the Oaken Torc. The spirit of Cunedda lingers around the torc, unable to find rest until one of his descendants assumes the throne. In the meantime, it defends the torc from anyone who might try to take it without the right. Treat the spirit as a wraith who can initiate Spirit Combat with anyone who touches the torc.

If the characters are present at the meeting of the council of the Einionydd, they may become aware of some cracks in the alliance of the Einionydd. Spotting some of these requires making a successful Insight roll, cajoling a retainer into unguarded speech with a successful Influence roll, or divining these through other means:

- ⚔ Prince Benlli's absence is not unusual. He rarely attends gatherings of the council these days.

- ⚔ Owain pays little attention to proceedings and is rarely asked for his input. His eyes drawn instead to the courtyard where Caer Segeint's warband are sparring with one another.

- ⚔ There is tension between Dogfeil and Cadwallon. Dogfeil always tries to find fault with his nephew's words; Cadwallon is tired of Dogfeil not following his leadership.

Moccus begins by clarifying the conditions of kingship (page 5) and wants to hear the arguments why a prince of the Einionydd should become king. He also asks them to list any unforgivable acts of the Ceredigydd: ones that would need some form of reparations before peace could be obtained. This is by far the longest part of proceedings. Most critically for Arthur, Moccus asks what it would take for them to join the Alliance of Britain. The Einionydd reveal their public goals: a Christian Gwynedd, the recapture of Afflogion from the Blackshield Irish, and a descendant of Einion on the throne.

Moccus has no authority to address these issues, but he does ask if there are any actions the Ceredigydd could do to bring the Einionydd to the negotiating table. Cadwallon asks the body of their favourite saint to be returned to them; Saint Dwynwen (see box) was taken from her resting place in Arfon during a raid several years ago. Meirion's uncle Maelon is presumed to be the instigator of this raid. However, Dwynwen's second wish cured Maelon of his passion for her: in fact, he never loved again despite marrying and having a son. Rather, Maelodd ap Maelon stole Dwynwen's body in a misguided attempt to get approval from his uncaring father.

The Sword of Dynod

Before they leave, Cadwallon asks to see the characters. On the table before him is a magnificent sword. Cunedda gave each of his sons a sword to mark their birth, and when his uncle Afloyg died, amongst his possessions was the Sword of Dynod, claimed when Dynod was killed in a skirmish on the border between their principalities. Cadwallon himself bears Afloyg's sword and Owain carries the one given to Einion.

In the interests of restoring peace between Cunedda's descendants, Cadwallon offers to return the sword to the sons of Dynod. He asks if the characters will travel to Dolbenmaen and deliver the Sword to Eifion ap Dynod on his behalf. A successful Customs roll tells the characters that by rights, the

St Dwynwen

A daughter of Saint Brychan (Mythic Britain, page 147) and the most beautiful of them all. She fell in love with Maelon, the brother of Meirion's mother, but when she rebuffed his sexual advances (wanting to wait until after marriage), he grew enraged and tried to force himself upon her. Dwynwen prayed to God for deliverance, and Maelon was turned into a block of ice. An angel came to Dwynwen in a dream and offered her three wishes as a reward for her chastity. She first wished that Maelon be turned back into flesh. Her second wish was that all true-hearted lovers should either obtain the objects of their affection or else be cured of their passion. Her final wish was that she should never have to marry, and true enough, she died in a hermitage in Arfon. She has become the patron saint of lovers amongst the Christians of Western Britain.

Miracles
Dismiss Magic, *Entangle* (actually turns target into ice with the same game effects), *Pacify*.

sword belongs to Dingad, the current Prince of Dunodion, not to his younger brother. If challenged on this, Cadwallon says that Dingad's behaviour towards the Einionydd has been particularly deplorable; besides, Eifion has just reached his majority and such an occasion deserves a gift.

In truth, Cadwallon is making overtures towards Eifion. He has reason to believe the princeling will be more amenable towards an alliance than his brother would and intends to replace Dingad with Eifion as prince of Dunodion if his plan bears fruit.

The Sword of Dynod

CELTIC GAMES

Many of these games involve the consumption of alcoholic drinks. Intoxication is treated like a poison that inflicts the Exhaustion Condition; each intoxicating dose (not necessarily the same as each drink) requires a new Endurance roll. Alcoholic drinks in Mythic Britain typically have a Potency of 20–50%.

Speed drinking: Simply, who can drink fastest. Make opposed Endurance rolls; the winner finishes first. Anyone failing the roll makes an immediate intoxication roll at Hard difficulty.

Gorhoffedd: Contestants take it in turns to take a drink (equivalent to an intoxicating dose of alcohol) and then recite a verse from a famous poem. The loser is the first person to make a mistake in their recitation. Each turn, make an Endurance roll opposed by the Potency of the drink. Then make a Customs roll for the recitation, penalised by the current state of intoxication. If the character would have succeeded if it had not been for the intoxication penalty, they are only disqualified if all their opponents succeed.

Capacity drinking: A less-sophisticated version of the Gorhoffedd, this game replaces the poetry with a physical task — balancing a mug on the head, standing on one foot, and so on — necessitating an Athletics (or possibly Brawn or Acrobatics) instead.

Throwboard: This is a dice game of pure luck. Each character puts in a monetary stake and rolls against their (POW5)%. All characters who succeed share the pot between them; a Critical Success counts as two shares. Some argue that successfully cheating at throwboard is the most important part of the game. See the rules under the Gambling skill (Mythras, page 46).

Badger-in-the-bag / Broch ygkot: A favourite (if cruel) game amongst the British. A live badger is put into a leather bag. Two opponents are armed with staves, and they take turns to strike the bag with their foot or the stick, trying to get it to their goal, which are set at opposite ends of the hall, 5–10 metres apart. They may only use the stick three times each in total. Each opponent makes an Unarmed roll, a Success moves the bag a number of metres equal to half the Damage roll (1d3 for a foot, 1d6 for the stick, plus any Damage Modifier) in whichever direction they wish.

REACTIVE EVENTS

IF WITH SAOIRSE AND TIORRACH

The principal mission of the Blackshield spies is to gain entrance to Caer Segeint and assess its defences. By accompanying the characters, Saoirse and Tiorrach have greater access than they had ever hoped. They make sure they see every part of the fort, including its earthworks. Tiorrach thinks they should attempt to kill Cadwallon or Owain while here. Saoirse argues this exceeds the orders Prince Connor gave them.

The characters might overhear the pair arguing about murder plans or be present when they make the attempt. The spies might encourage the characters to take Owain up on his offer of a boar hunt, since this gives them not only the opportunity but also the perfect cover. The Einionydd will look very poorly on the characters' delegation if any such plot should be uncovered, even if the characters are instrumental in foiling it. At the very least, the characters (as well as the spies) will be put on trial where they can argue their innocence.

As it happens, Connor mac Eird will not thank Saoirse and Tiorrach for their murder plot, successful or otherwise: the last thing he wants at the moment is open war with the Einionydd.

IF WITH GWRIN

If the characters have already visited the Ceredigydd, they likely have Gwrin in tow (page 40). During the eisteddfod, Queen Meredith interrupts proceedings asking for hush. A voice can be heard, a beautiful male voice singing a soulful lament somewhere in Caer Segeint. She orders a search of the fort until the singer can be found. The characters may take part in this hunt if they wish. Eventually, the singer is found

CELTIC GAMES

Cywydd y Fost: A major part of Celtic culture is to be proud of one's accomplishments and ancestors. The cywydd y fost is a boasting contest, where each contestant tries to top their opponent's boast with a better one of their own, typically in verse. The winner is judged by the audience. Resolve the contest with opposed Oratory rolls (Influence can be substituted at a Hard penalty). Each round, the character can augment their roll with another skill applicable to a particular exploit or ancestor: Art (Poetry), Deceit, Insight, Lore (Celtic), Lore (Strategy and Tactics), and so forth. But, it must be a different skill each time — the audience gets bored quickly by similar boasts. The first to accumulate three Successes is judged the winner. A poetic debate (ymryson) or an insult contest (araith) can be conducted in the same way. Alternatively, use the rules for Social Conflicts (Mythic Companion, page 14) for all three of these competitions.

Wrestling: Celtic wrestling focusses on grips and throws rather than strikes. Each wrestler has four "pins" (the two shoulder blades and both buttocks) and a point is scored each time an opponent's "pin" touches the ground first in a fall. A "back" is scored if at least three of the four pins touch the ground at the same time. After any part of either opponent touches the ground (other than hands and feet), both opponents let go and regain their feet. A "back" wins the bout immediately; otherwise, the combat lasts 10 Rounds and the opponent with the most "pins" wins the bout.

A wrestling match is a combat using the Unarmed skill. A character scores a "pin" if they use the Trip Opponent Special Effect on their opponent and their opponent fails their resistance roll against the trip. If the opponent succeeds their resistance roll but rolls under the original attack roll, then they still trip over as normal, but touch the ground first with something other than one of their pins. A "back" is scored in the same way as a pin, but the opponent must have been held (with the Grip Special Effect) before they were tripped. If this is achieved in a single move (i.e., two levels of Success), then the wrestler gets a four-pin back, which is considered a more impressive move.

Fire jumping: Opponents jump between two staves with a bonfire in between. Those who fail an Athletics roll are eliminated (but not burned unless they Fumble); the staves are then pushed further apart and contestants jump again until there is one winner.

Gwyddbwyll (Mythic Britain, page 116): Differential Rolls of Customs or Gaming, augmented with Lore (Strategy and Tactics). The first player to accumulate four Successes is the winner.

— it is Gwrin, singing to himself while he completes some chore for the characters (cleaning a saddle, brushing a horse, or the like).

Gwrin is brought before the court and asked to sing again. With the eyes of the Einionydd on him, the boy makes a couple of false starts, but overcomes his nerves and manages a haunting rendition of the song. Meredith is entranced, tears rolling down her cheeks; others who have suffered loss are similarly affected, although watchful characters might spot a few jealous glances amongst the gathered performers. If any of the characters have the Trance skill, they may detect that Gwrin is temporarily possessed by an ancestor spirit, raising his Sing skill to 128% by the Sagacity Spirit Ability. There are no druids amongst the Einionydd, so without the characters, this remains unknown.

Queen Meredith insists that Gwrin stays with her at Caer Segeint, and the characters are not really in a position to refuse; although they might sell him rather than give him to the queen. Gwrin is happy to stay in Caer Segeint; he loves singing and would be happy to do so for the queen. If forced to admit it, he confesses he knows that the spirit of his grandmother takes him over when he sings, but sees no harm in it if it pleases others. Gwrin begs the characters not to reveal where they got him, for fear of spoiling the job opportunity. This is, of course, what Bleiddud intended all along. When, in the future, the characters hear of Queen Meredith's death and the weakening of the alliance between Powys and the Einionydd because of it, they may remember the lad they left in her care and wonder if they were a tool of the Ceredigydd.

TROUBLE IN MEIRIONYDD

Meirionydd is most easily approached from Powys in the south. It has no coast, being bordered by the salt marshes of Gwaelod in the west. Routes from the north or northeast involve travel through the valleys carved out by the River Mawddach.

As the characters approach Caer Aderyn, a warband lead by Morfran ap Typaun ambushes them. All the warriors are Picts and have stripped naked to reveal their fearsome tattoos. Morfran is a seasoned warrior; use the statistics of Gawain (Mythic Britain, page 210) and add the Love Battle Passion of 90%. His brother has summoned a nature (bear) spirit for him, blessing him with natural Armour Points. He has also taken Frenzy Root (page 12). The Picts have the statistics of Typical Warriors (Mythic Britain, page 213); they lack armour, although Morfran has shared the Frenzy Root with them via his spittle.

Just as the battle reaches its height (and hopefully before anyone is seriously injured), Bleiddud arrives on horseback with a bigger group of warriors who use their horses to break up the fight. Morfran is deep under the thrall of the Frenzy Root, and Bleiddud's men hold him down and force wine down his throat to counteract the poison. Bleiddud apologies for his uncle's behaviour and offers a blood-price (Mythic Britain, page 117) for any injuries inflicted. He also offers them hospitality on his father's behalf.

SPEARPOINT NEGOTIATIONS

Caer Aderyn is virtually hidden by the huge flock of red kites, carrion crows, and gulls that feast on the corpses hanging on iron hooks driven into its walls. A couple of the victims are still alive as the birds tear into their flesh. Bleiddud explains that the victims are Irish raiders; indeed, Morfran attacked the characters mistaking them for Blackshields.

Once within the ring fort, attendants show the characters to a guest house and tell them there will be a feast this evening. The noise and tumult of Meirion's feast hall will likely surprise the characters; this is no sedate courtly affair typical at a chieftain's table elsewhere in Britain. Meirion and his kin sit amongst the warriors and there is little in the way of formality. Meirion glares at his guests with open suspicion throughout the meal and ignores all attempts at conversation. Morvan whispers in his ear the whole time, and since his twin is absent, the characters may not realise that this is not the man they fought in battle. Bleiddud does his best to be the charming host in the face of his father's rudeness.

Midway through the feast, Meirion demands all the food is taken away and the tables cleared. He wants to know why the characters are here. This is the cue for Felimid to step up, but the bard may not have realised his skills would be called upon so soon and may have been indulging in the mead and wine. Make a Passion (Love Self-Indulgence) roll for him opposed against his Willpower; Failure means that he has a level of Fatigue from intoxication. Meirion seems intent at finding fault with whatever Felimid says; the prince seems particularly incensed that Arthur would send him an envoy who knows nothing of battle. He states he is willing to bet Felimid doesn't know one end of a spear from the other. Morvan stands and declares he will take the bet. It is clear this situation has been engineered to make the characters fight. Meirion picks a warrior from amongst the Ceredigydd to fight Felimid, and the gathered warriors form a circle in which the duel will take place.

If the characters act quick enough (and a successful Courtesy roll helps), they can remind Bleiddud (who is clearly not party to his father's and uncle's game) that Felimid is a guest and one of the Aes Dana. Bleiddud seizes on this and persuades his father to let the bard choose a champion. If the characters have been accommodating guests — especially given the rocky start — then the opponent is a young warrior with something to prove; otherwise, it is one of the clan's champions. No terms of the fight are set unless the characters think to mention them, but the Ceredigydd are intent on humiliating the outsiders rather than killing them, and their champion withholds any lethal blows and concentrates on disarming and tripping manoeuvres.

Taking part in the duel indicates the willingness of the negotiators to listen to the Ceredigydd case. If there are Wounds to patch up, then talks are scheduled to start on the following day. At that time, it is just Bleiddud and his advisors, with neither his father nor uncles making an appearance. Bleiddud outlines the public goals of the Ceredigydd faction: to recapture Afflogion, to defeat Cadwallon and Owain, and to install Meirion as king of Gwynedd.

These are uncompromising goals, but Bleiddud also mentions several issues that might at least bring the Ceredigydd to the negotiating table. One of these is payment of the blood-price (Mythic Britain, page 117) for the death of Dynod 12 years ago. A Ceredigydd warrior who survived the skirmish swears that Dynod did not die in battle, but that Afloyg executed him after his capture. The Ceredigydd will accept the surrender of Afflogion in remittance of this debt, arguing that occupation by the Blackshield Irish greatly diminishes its current value. They may be willing to accept a portion of the cantref as long as it is greater than the portion left to the Einionydd. The Ceredigydd claim hinges upon the testimony of a single individual, who is oath-sworn to them, but there may be other witnesses, such as some of the warriors formerly sworn to Afloyg who now serve in Cadwallon's warband. Bleiddud tasks the characters with uncovering the truth of this decade-old crime.

REPAYING THE DEBT

Bleiddud apologises once again for his family's actions. He pays them the fine for the assault committed by Morfran: even if the characters suffered no injury, they did suffer insult and he would be no lord if he did not recompense their honour. This takes the form of silver jewellery and a horse, plus a slave to look after it. If the characters are already suspicious, then allow them a Hard Insight roll to see a significant look pass between Bleiddud and the slave.

The slave's name is Gwrin; he is 14 years old, and secretly Bleiddud's nephew and stepson. He keeps his tattoos — one for every year of his life —hidden by clothing, for they reveal his noble blood. He wears a torc around his neck, a cheap thing of copper, but it has been handed down the generations and allows the spirit of Gwrin's mother's mother to find him from the World of Spirits. Gwrin has no power to see or summon her, but can sometimes sense that she is watching over him.

Gwrin is a quiet and unassuming boy, who seems eager to be out in the world at last. He keeps up the pretence of being a slave; although, if the characters probe too much he "confesses" he might be Bleiddud's bastard. Gwrin latches on to one of the characters — the one with the highest status or greatest renown as a warrior — and becomes their body slave: carrying their gear, washing their clothes, fetching their meals, all with a shy smile. He often hums to himself while completing his chores. Despite his age, Gwrin is an accomplished liar and actor.

Gwrin's role is to get close to Meredith, Cunedda's queen and Einion's mother. His mission is to eventually kill her, but only when the time is right for the Ceredigydd. If the characters have yet to visit Caer Segeint, then he accompanies them there and plays upon the queen's well-known weakness for music to get close to her. If the characters have already visited Caer Segeint, then his best bet is to be captured by the Blackshield Irish and then convince them to sell him to the Einionydd as a hostage rather than ransom him back to the Ceredigydd.

REACTIVE EVENTS

IF WITH SAOIRSE AND TIORRACH

Having seen Caer Aderyn and its treatment of their compatriots, the two Irishmen are keen to leave at the earliest opportunity. They know one or two of the people hanging on the fort's outer wall and have no desire to join them. They plan to sneak out under the cover of darkness. Unless the characters take special precautions overnight — out of paranoia for their general predicament or specifically out of suspicion of Saoirse and Tiorrach — the pair escape without incident. Their sudden disappearance looks very bad for the characters, and they may have to talk very fast to avoid the crazed and paranoid Meirion imprisoning and possibly executing them as spies.

IF CARRYING THE SWORD OF DYNOD

Unless the characters show the sword to their hosts or give them a reason to search the characters' belongings, the Sword of Dynod remains hidden. However, if it becomes known they are carrying the sword, then they have questions to answer. The sword is instantly recognised — Meirion has a similar one given to his father Typaun — and it was known to be in the possession of the Einionydd ever since Dynod was killed in a border skirmish in Afflogion 12 years ago led by his half-brother Afloyg. The characters are hauled before Meirion, who demands to know how they have his uncle's sword — and their explanation had better be good. Bleiddud's calming influence might be able to prevent them from being fed alive to the fort's carrion birds, but only if they agree to become his agents. He asks them for oaths to this effect, relying on the characters' adherence to the Celtic ideal of honour (Mythic Britain, page 99). As their first task, he asks them to deliver the sword to Eifion as planned, but to make it clear that it has been returned to him by Bleiddud rather than Cadwallon. He also sends them to deliver Gwrin to Caer Segeint, but with no need to keep Gwrin's identity a secret. At the Games Masters' discretion, Bleiddud may set the characters more tasks before he considers their life-debt paid in full.

VISITING DOLBENMAEN

Eifion ap Dynod calls Dolbenmaen home, a small circle fort on an isolated hill with a river running past it to the north. It is a difficult place to reach and an easy place to defend. The characters have no real reason to visit Eifion unless they were given the Sword of Dynod by Cadwallon. For the purposes of the story, it is preferable for the characters to still have the sword when they visit one of the other princes, so their reception at Dolbenmaen depends on their point of departure.

If the characters come here directly from Caer Segeint, they find that Eifion is not currently at home. Cichol (the captain of Eifion's warband) is cautious of some Einionydd ruse; in the interests of hospitality, he'll offer the characters basic fare but not admit them into the hillfort. He cannot (or will not) say how long his lord will be gone, only that it could be a week or more. After three days, provisions from

Dolbenmaen dry up, indicating that the characters have overstayed their welcome.

If the characters come to Dolbenmaen via another route, then they find Eifion in residence. The lordling is young — just 18 years old — but has ruled for four years. He is genuinely pleased to receive his father's sword, but immediately recognises it as an effort of the Einionydd to court his favour. Understandably, he mistakes the characters for Cadwallon's agents and asks what news they bring from the prince. If they realise Eifion's mistake (requiring an Insight roll) and successfully play along with the ruse (requiring Deceit, Acting, or Influence rolls), then they learn Eifion has had prior contact with the Einionydd. On Cadwallon's advice, he did not take part in a recent Ceredigydd raid on Rhufoniog, a raid for which the Einionydd had prior knowledge and were waiting for the invaders in the mountain pass.

While at Dolbenmaen (whether they meet Eifion immediately or not), they encounter another visitor to the hillfort: Bolg, an agent for the Venedoti (page 17). He stands out because his dress and appearance mark him as an Ordovices, although a Formidable Lore (Celt) roll identifies him instead as one of the aboriginal people of Gwynedd through subtle clues like the style of his belt buckles and the lacing on his boots. Either way he stands out as unusual in this Ceredigydd household. After they first meet him, the characters may have several more encounters where they spot Bolg spying on them. Although as soon as he realises that his attention has been noticed, Bolg departs Dolbenmaen immediately. If put to the question, Bolg claims to be a representative from a hamlet near the headwaters of the River Dwyryd, looking for buyers for their sheep. Eifion professes not to know Bolg (the spy has not yet made contact) and refers the characters to Cichol, who merely repeats Bolg's cover story.

In the future, if Eifion usurps his brother's rule and declares for the Einionydd, the characters might realise the small part they played in bringing this about.

The Island Prince

If the characters want to visit Osmaeliog, then they need a ship. The dangers of the Blackshield Irish in the seas around Gwynedd should be made clear prior to departure. The characters may have to buy boats to make the journey or at least put down a pricy surety against the chance that they don't return. They may have difficulty finding a crew willing to make the journey and have to use all their persuasive powers to make it happen. They may be able to recoup some of the cost if they take on cargo; goods long overdue in Osmaeliog include wool, grain, pottery, and glass ingots.

If the characters are travelling from Arfon, Caer Segeint is a port on the estuary of the River Seiont, and if the characters have remained on good terms with the Einionydd, Cadwallon arranges for a boat to take them to his cousin. It is marginally safer travelling from Caer Segeint, since the ship can hug the coast and remain hidden. But they cannot seek shelter on the coast of Ynys Mon. Whereas, sailing from Caer Wyddno offers the Afflogion coast, with its numerous coves that could be used to escape from pursuers.

From Caer Aderyn, the closest suitable port is Caer Wyddno, which allows the characters to visit the home of a significant ally of the Ceredigydd, although there is little diplomatic business to complete here as Gwyddno has publicly counted himself out of the running for King of Gwynedd — at least for now.

Dangerous Waters

Whichever way they go, the characters encounter the Blackshield Irish on the sea. A lone ship with black sails is sighted, at a distance that depends very much on the characters' route and use of the coastline. The Irish pirates are expert sailors and pursues the characters' boat. Rules for Chases can be found in the Mythras Companion (page 41); alternatively, this could be run as a series of Differential Rolls on the Seamanship skill, with each level of Success representing a change in the relative distance between the vessels. Decide on the lead the characters have when the encounter starts (for example, 5 Successes). If the Irish close the lead to 1 Success, they can commence missile combat, and at 0 Successes, they can board. The characters get away if they open the lead to 10 or more Successes. Finegal, the captain of the Blackshield ship, has a Seamanship of 75%.

If the pirates get close enough to board, then any local crewmembers immediately surrender, having learned that the Irish are less interested in killing people as they are in cargo and valuables. But the pirates are ruthless if given any resistance. Should it come to a fight, treat the 10 pirates as Typical Warriors (Mythic Britain, page 213) and Finegal as a Typical Young Chieftain (Mythic Britain, page 205) but in scale armour rather than mail. They have the Excellent Footwork Combat Style Trait rather than Shieldwall.

Reactive Events

If With Saoirse and Tiorrach

Finegal recognises his fellow Irishmen and immediately blows their cover. If the characters have treated the two spies decently, Saoirse intervenes with Finegal and the boat escapes unscathed. However, once revealed, the pair have to leave with the Irish; they will be put to death by Elnaw if any of the boat's crew reveals their identity.

IF WITH GWRIN

Gwrin's tattoos — although he tries to keep them hidden — betray him as a high-status Pict and thus potentially worth a large ransom. If Saoirse and Tiorrach are present and have no loyalty to the characters, then they tell Finegal about him (Gwrin's status might be news to the characters as well!). Keeping Gwrin out of the hands of the pirates probably requires a fight.

IF CARRYING THE SWORD OF DYNOD

If Finegal finds the Sword of Dynod after searching the characters' ship, then he confiscates it unless Saoirse intervenes on their behalf. If they try to hide it — or any other goods — prior to boarding, match the character's Conceal roll with the pirates' average Perception of 64%. The only way to retain possession of the sword once it has been found is to defeat Finegal and his crew.

CAER GYBI

Osmaeliog has a small fishing hamlet on the west coast called Towyn, which serves as its port; there is then a short overland journey to Caer Gybi. This old Roman fort has only three walls; the fourth side is fronted by the sea. There is a watchtower in the town and another within its line of sight on the mountainside, two and a half kilometres to the west.

At Caer Gybi, the characters receive a warm welcome from Elnaw ap Osfael. There are so few visitors to his island that he is pleased for the company, especially in the form of adventurers from distant lands. He is keen to update his information on Britain — current rulers, royal marriages and births, changes in significant lords, and so forth — and calls in three bards to memorise the answers to his questions. He is particularly interested in the Alliance of Britain and who joined it. This might be a real test of the players' knowledge (helped by their characters' skills, of course)!

In return, Elnaw is happy to answer questions about the situation in Gwynedd. He can describe his grandfather's conditions for kingship and outline the other two factions. He'll outline his own goals (all are public), professing that, while he does not seek the kingship himself, he would accept it if (and only if) it guaranteed peace between his kin.

Elnaw mentions a problem with which the characters may be able to help. Ever since the conquest of Afflogion by the Blackshield Irish, there has been a small colony of refugees on the south end of the island. He has had reports that the village is stockpiling weapons and training in their use in preparation of the reinvasion of Afflogion. Elnaw fears he will be obligated to provide assistance, but even with his help, they have no chance against the Blackshield Irish. The situation is too delicate for him to approach them directly and asks the characters to pay them a visit and let him know what they find. The villagers are indeed arming for war — just not the war that Elnaw thinks. The village has been infiltrated by Irishmen masquerading as Britons, and most of the families in the village are now loyal to Connor mac Eird. They are preparing to seize control of the island on his behalf, mounting an assault against Caer Gybi while Osmaeliog's warband is occupied with a raiding party of Blackshield Irish.

While at Caer Gybi, the characters might be approached (independently) by Morcanwg and Prior Dafyn (page 15). Both are loyal to their prince, but are concerned that Elnaw is still unmarried. He cannot take a bride from amongst the princesses of Western Britain without losing his neutral position, and they ask if Arthur might be able to suggest a suitable match. Guinevere's sister Gwenhyfach would seem to be a good option; once Guinevere and Arthur are married, this would create an alliance between Osmaeliog and Dumnonia. In fact, Gwenhyfach's paternal grandfather was the brother of Elnaw's paternal grandmother, making them second cousins. Gwenhyfach's father Cywyrd knows this, but cannot reveal the kinship without also betraying his family's secret, that his father Cynfawr was the last King of Rhos.

CONCLUSION

A united Gwynedd is no closer at the conclusion of this adventure than it was at the start, but the characters know a lot more about the complex situation in this divided land. They can report to Arthur that the Einionydd are riven with indecision, the Ceredigydd are cursed with madness, and the Osmaeliog are impotent.

The characters may have changed the balance among the factions in some small way over the course of the adventure. Make sure the characters are aware of the shifting patterns of politics their actions caused: explain that a goal is expressed as a percentage and tell them how many points their characters have earned for that faction, but do not reveal the resulting goal score. The following are some goals to track:

- If Saint Dwynwen's relics are returned, advance the Einionydd goal to stamp out the pagan faith.

- If Eifion has the Sword of Dynod, advance the Einionydd goal to install him as prince of Dunodion.

- If Saoirse and Tiorrach try to kill either of the Einionydd princes, then decrease the Blackshield Irish goal to secure a truce with the rulers of Gwynedd.

- If Gwrin is in the court of Cadwallon, advance the Ceredigydd goal to conquer Caer Segeint.

- If a blood-price is agreed for the death of Dynod, advance the Ceredigydd goal to convince Benlli to swap sides (he sees this as a weakness in the Einionydd faction).

- If the Irish attack on Caer Gybi is foiled, advance the Osmaelydd goal to defeat the Blackshields.

- If a wife is found for Elnaw outside of Western Britain, advance the Osmaelydd goal to secure stability for the cantref.

If the characters want to continue to adventure in Gwynedd, they can begin the long struggle to undo two decades of hatred, betrayal, and strife. They may decide to join either the Einionydd or Ceredigydd faction, having decided which of the princes would best serve Britain as King of Gwynedd. They might instead join with Elnaw to try to find a compromise that is best for Gwynedd. If the characters spoke to the key factions, then they should be aware that the Ceredigydd, the Einionydd, and the Osmaelydd all seek the elimination of the Blackshield Irish. Coordinating a joint action against the invaders would not be an easy task, but it could be the common cause that opens the door towards future cooperation.

The characters could also start their own faction, dedicated to bringing Gwynedd into the Alliance of Britain, united or not. Its resources would begin small, consisting of whatever the characters bring plus whatever Arthur can spare. Its goals might include be dealing with the Blackshield Irish, forging political marriages between the two clans, and/or lessening the religious divide. The true coup would be to get both the Ceredigydd and the Einionydd to join the Alliance; uniting under a common cause might start to heal the rift between the clans.

Non-Player Characters

Felimid the Bard

A short, slight man, with a quick smile and friendly eyes. He prefers to go beardless, which gives him a boyish charm, although he wears full sideburns to advertise his maturity. Felimid typically wears a green cape over red braecci and a white tunic covered with intricate interwoven embroidery. He has tattoos of sunwheels on the backs of both hands. He is never far from his harp, which he carries in a waterproof case. When necessary, he carries a willow branch stripped of its bark, which announces his status as a bard and envoy.

Characteristics	Attributes
STR: 7	Action Points: 3
CON: 8	Damage Modifier: −1d2
SIZ: 9	Magic Points: 12
DEX: 14	Movement: 6 metres
INT: 12	Initiative Bonus: +13 (−2 for armour)= +11
POW: 12	Armour: Reinforced leather helm, leather tunic, hide trousers
CHA: 15	

Skills: Acting 40%, Art (Poetry) 72%, Athletics 26%, Brawn 21%, Courtesy 42%, Endurance 31%, Evade 33%, First Aid 31%, Gambling 39%, Influence 40%, Insight 54%, Locale 29%, Lore (Britain) 44%, Lore (Celt) 79%, Lore (Myths) 44%, Lore (Pagan) 49%, Musicianship (stringed instruments) 59%, Oratory 57%, Perception 34%, Seduction 32%, Sing 67%, Superstition 41%, Survival 27%, Unarmed 21%, Willpower 44%

Passions: Loyal to Britain 57%, Loyal to Arthur 52%, Love Self-Indulgence 64%, Hate Saxons 54%, Pagan 57%

1d20	Location	AP/HP
01–03	Right Leg	1/4
04–16	Left Leg	1/4
07–09	Abdomen	2/5
10–12	Chest	2/6
13–15	Right Arm	0/3
16–18	Left Arm	0/3
19–20	Head	3/4

Combat Style: Warrior (Spear, Sword and Shield) 41%

Weapon	Size (Force)	Reach	Damage	AP/HP
Shortspear	M	L	1d8+1−1d2	4/5

Moccus the Monk

A bulky man with a large nose. His clumsiness has become a joke amongst his fellow monks. He has a monastic tonsure and no facial hair, and wears a pale brown habit and darker cloak, both of which are often travel-stained. He carries a leather satchel with a psalter, stylus, wax tablet, and other essentials. Moccus is sharp-witted, and while pious, he does not flaunt his faith or evangelise to pagans.

Characteristics	Attributes
STR: 9	Action Points: 2
CON: 14	Damage Modifier: 0
SIZ: 12	Magic Points: 8
DEX: 7	Movement: 6 metres
INT: 15	Initiative Bonus: +11
POW: 8	Armour: None
CHA: 12	Magic: Christian Miracles

Skills: Art (illumination) 30%, Athletics 26%, Brawn 26%, Courtesy 37%, Craft (books) 22%, Deceit 32%, Devotion 35%, Endurance 53%, Evade 39%, First Aid 52%, Influence 59%, Insight 43%, Language (Latin) 42%, Literacy 45%, Locale 50%, Lore (Celt) 75%, Lore (Christian) 60%, Oratory 50%, Perception 33%, Sing 30%, Superstition 14%, Survival 35%, Teach 32%, Unarmed 26%, Willpower 41%

Passions: Loyal to Abbot 53%, Loyal to Queen Elliw 48%, Love Peace 46%, Hate Injustice 46%, Christian 63%

1d20	Location	AP/HP
01–03	Right Leg	0/6
04–16	Left Leg	0/6
07–09	Abdomen	0/7
10–12	Chest	0/8
13–15	Right Arm	0/5
16–18	Left Arm	0/5
19–20	Head	0/6

Combat Style: Warrior (Spear, Sword and Shield) 31%

Weapon	Size (Force)	Reach	Damage	AP/HP
Shield	H	S	1d3+1	5/15

SAOIRSE (IRISH SPY)

Lanky, with a mop of fair hair and bright, blue eyes, and blessed with an infectious, jovial laugh that encourages people to take him into their confidence, Saoirse is easy to talk to and easy to like. He's also highly perceptive and has a keen eye for the human weakness, and has no qualms about exploiting it. For all his likability and easy charm, he despises most people and even relishes using them.

Characteristics	Attributes
STR: 9	Action Points: 3
CON: 11	Damage Modifier: 0
SIZ: 9	Magic Points: 8
DEX: 14	Movement: 6 metres
INT: 13	Initiative Bonus: +14
POW: 8	Armour: None
CHA: 10	

Skills: Athletics 34%, Brawn 25%, Courtesy 51%, Deceit 65%, Endurance 33%, Evade 36%, Influence 65%, Insight 60%, Locale 28%, Lore (Ireland) 44%, Lore (Celt) 36%, Perception 60%, Superstition 51%, Unarmed 36%, Willpower 58%

Passions: Loyal to Ireland 77%, Loyal to Blackshields 67%, Love Intrigue 64%, Christian 57%

1d20	Location	AP/HP
01–03	Right Leg	0/4
04–16	Left Leg	0/4
07–09	Abdomen	0/5
10–12	Chest	0/6
13–15	Right Arm	0/3
16–18	Left Arm	0/3
19–20	Head	0/4

Combat Style: Warrior (Spear, Sword and Shield) 52%

Weapon	Size (Force)	Reach	Damage	AP/HP
Shortspear	M	L	1d8+1	4/5

TIORRACH (IRISH SPY)

As dour as Saoirse is endearing, Tiorrach has a head for numbers, deals, bargains, and the merits of well-made plans. While Saoirse works on people, Tiorrach works on surroundings. He can quickly assess the viability of fortifications, guard rosters, defences, and identify weaknesses, openings and points of vulnerability. He is a head shorter than Saoirse, with an imposing mono-brow over downward-drooping eyes. Tiorrach even appears to be a little slow-witted, although he is anything but.

Characteristics	Attributes
STR: 11	Action Points: 3
CON: 10	Damage Modifier: 0
SIZ: 9	Magic Points: 10
DEX: 16	Movement: 6 metres
INT: 14	Initiative Bonus: +15
POW: 10	Armour: None
CHA: 7	

Skills: Athletics 28%, Brawn 36%, Deceit 44%, Endurance 30%, Evade 48%, Influence 37%, Insight 70%, Locale 52%, Lore (Ireland) 60%, Lore (Celt) 44%, Lore (Strategy & Tactics) 64%, Mechanisms 36%, Perception 72%, Superstition 77%, Unarmed 36%, Willpower 30%

Passions: Loyal to Ireland 64%, Loyal to Blackshields 64%, Love Plans 67%, Christian 60%

1d20	Location	AP/HP
01–03	Right Leg	0/4
04–16	Left Leg	0/4
07–09	Abdomen	0/5
10–12	Chest	0/6
13–15	Right Arm	0/3
16–18	Left Arm	0/3
19–20	Head	0/4

Combat Style: Warrior (Spear, Sword and Shield 52%

Weapon	Size (Force)	Reach	Damage	AP/HP
Shortspear	M	L	1d8+1	4/5

GWRIN AP CADWALADR

On the cusp of adulthood, Gwrin takes care to cover his tattoos, and wears a cheap band of copper around his thin neck. Quiet almost to the point of shyness, Gwrin can easily fade from attention simply by sitting silently in a corner, listening and watching. Few give him a second glance, and he is careful not give anyone cause. As noted, he attaches himself to the character with the highest apparent status as a warrior, making himself their lackey.

Characteristics	Attributes
STR: 9	Action Points: 2
CON: 12	Damage Modifier: -1d2
SIZ: 11	Magic Points: 10
DEX: 10	Movement: 6 metres
INT: 13	Initiative Bonus: +12
POW: 10	Armour: None
CHA: 15	Magic: Ancestral Spirit (see below)

Skills: Acting 50%, Art (Poetry) 35%, Athletics 39%, Brawn 25%, Deceit 58%, Endurance 44%, Evade 30%, Influence 45%, Insight 38%, Locale (Meirionydd) 31%, Lore (Pagan) 31%, Musicianship 35%, Oratory 35%, Perception 33%, Sing 55%, Superstition 42%, Survival 40%, Unarmed 39%, Willpower 30%

Passions: Loyal to Bleiddud 55%, Loyal to Ceredigydd 50%, Love Mother 50%, Hate Einionydd 50%, Pagan 55%

Arianhad, an ancestor spirit; INT 14, POW 16, CHA 15; Customs 128%, Lore (Gwynedd) 128%, Spectral Combat 87%, Willpower 86%; Sagacity (Deceit), Sagacity (Musicianship), Sagacity (Sing), Spellcasting (Incognito, Voice)

1d20	Location	AP/HP
01–03	Right Leg	0/5
04–16	Left Leg	0/5
07–09	Abdomen	0/6
10–12	Chest	0/7
13–15	Right Arm	0/4
16–18	Left Arm	0/4
19–20	Head	0/5

Combat Style: Warrior (Spear, Sword and Shield) 39%

Weapon	Size (Force)	Reach	Damage	AP/HP
Shortspear	M	L	1d8+1+1d2	4/5

GWYNEDD CAMPAIGNS

This section contains some ideas for further stories set in Gwynedd, outside of the feud between the clans.

The Coat of Beisrydd

Cunedda was the grandson of Padarn Beisrydd, who was the last known owner of the Coat of Beisrydd, one of the Treasures of Britain. If running the Mythic Britain Campaign, rather than Merlin simply telling the characters that the Coat lies in the Caves of the Circind (Mythic Britain, pages 296–313), he could instead send them to Gwynedd to try to find what happened to it. This would introduce the characters to the quarrelling descendants of Padarn as they try to navigate the turmoil towards someone who knows its fate. Elnaw of Osmaeliog is the most likely to know that it was stolen from Cunedda's father Adern by the Circind Votadini and is now the property of Mawgaus. Alternatively, Elnaw might not know but suggests they consult the Head of Bran the Blessed, providing a link to that story seed (page 47).

The Flooding of Maes Gwyddno

The floodgates on Gwaelod's sea wall are normally left open to refresh the water in Gwaelod, but once a month, the tides are too strong and the lord of Caer Rihog, Seithenyn Hen, must close the gates. Seithenyn hosts a feast to celebrate his own importance on the night in question. When Seithenyn is left unable to close the gates, the whole of the Maes Gwyddno is under threat of destruction by the floodwaters.

Note this adventure recreates the events of a real 6th-century story. To preserve the legend, the Games Master might choose to make stopping the flood impossible and direct the characters instead towards saving its inhabitants.

Background

Mererid is the daughter of Gwyddno and is being fostered at Caer Rihog. She fell victim to Seithenyn's drunken lust and seeks revenge on him. A one-eyed washerwoman (actually Eithne in disguise, see page 22) gave her the idea that if Seithenyn was too drunk to close the floodgates, he would be publicly shamed, perhaps even stripped of his rank. Eithne offers Mererid a poison to stupefy the lord, although the dose she provides is enough to be fatal. The druid knows a particularly high tide is due, enough to overcome the seawalls and obliterate the Maes Gwyddno if the gates remain open.

Hook

The characters are staying at Caer Rihog, perhaps as part of a diplomatic mission or perhaps sheltering against the raging storm. Seithenyn is a notorious drunkard and his obnoxious conduct while inebriated makes his guests uncomfortable. He boasts about his vitally important role to Gwaelod, showing off the key he wears around his neck as a badge of his rank.

As an alternative scenario, the characters may discover Eithne's plot ahead of time and bring it to their faction leaders, only to be told to keep the information to themselves: both of the major factions would like to see the son of Ceredig diminished as he is a potential threat to their own causes. The characters must decide whether to go against the wishes of their faction to save the lives of strangers.

ACTION & EVENTS

The characters might witness Mererid talking with Eithne or see her put something in the lord's wine. Alternatively, they could be with Seithenyn when he collapses. Poison should be easy to diagnose, either from Seithenyn's symptoms or the fatal effects of feeding the untasted wine to an animal. Discovering the poisoner and/or the motive for the poisoning should be harder to discover.

Immediately after the poisoning attempt, both Mererid and Eithne leave Caer Rihog in different directions without even waiting to discover whether the plot succeeded. Mererid steals a horse and heads south towards Caer Wyddno and her father. She is distraught, both by the abuse she has suffered and the action she has taken. If the characters catch up with her, she confesses her part without inducement. Her intent was never to kill Seithenyn but only to embarrass him. She has no idea how devastating her actions might prove for her father's lands.

Eithne heads east at an unconcerned pace. She doesn't bother maintaining her washerwoman guise and resorts to blatant displays of magic to intimidate any who try to put her to the question. Like many druids, she considers her actions ordained by the gods and beyond mortal reproach. She does, however, warn the characters that they should not be wasting time with her when the Maes Gwyddno is under dire threat.

CLIMAX

The floodgates are wide open and the sea is flooding in. What's more, the storm that has been brewing all night is now battering the coast with gale-force winds. The characters are forced to make a choice — close the gates or save the people at risk; there is no time to do both.

If the characters try to stop the flood, it is a race to the sea walls ahead of the tide and force the gates closed against the incoming tide. The gates are massive edifices of tarred wood operated by Roman-engineered gears and ratchets. Hopefully the characters have thought to bring the key — not the symbolic one that Seithenyn wears around his neck, but the metre-long toothed iron bar that operates the floodgates. Even then, closing the gates as the sea presses against them requires a Herculean effort, requiring a dozen people to work in concert with one another. Debris brought up from the sea bottom by the inrushing tide may block the gates, needing a hero to dive down to knock it free or attach a rope with which it can be hauled away.

The characters may instead try to rescue the inhabitants of the 16 settlements on the Maes Gwyddno. The incoming tide takes fewer than three hours to flood the entire plain; the water rises faster than a person can walk. There are plenty of opportunities for peril and heroics:

- A child has climbed up onto the roof of their house, but the floodwaters are eroding the wattle and daub walls.

- An elderly couple cling together as they move at their fastest pace away but neither is faster than the rising tide.

- A person sits in a two-person coracle, yelling frantically at two people fighting each other to join them. One is their spouse, the other their sibling, and their struggles threaten both the boat and the person in it.

- A nurse has taken two of Gwyddno's sons — Rhun (aged 8) and Dyfnwal (aged 6) — for a ride, along with a single member of the warband. They are now stranded on a levy with panicking horses.

- Mererid took a shortcut across the Maes Gwyddno and is now trapped. Her horse has drowned, and she is clinging onto its corpse as it gets buffeted by the tumultuous currents.

CONSEQUENCES

If flood inundates Maes Gwyddno, 12 settlements are submerged by the floodwaters and hundreds of people lose their lives. The flood is a blow to Powys, since much of its gold comes from Gwaelod. The Ceredigydd also suffer from the diminishment of an ally, but that just makes them more dependent on Siluria for assistance and more likely to accede to King Iuchar's demands — exactly what Eithne planned.

If the characters' save Gwaelod's plain, then Gwyddno owes them a huge debt. He may even consider them for the lordship of Caer Rihog if Seithenyn did not survive the poisoning. They might also attract the attention of Eithne, who wants revenge for her spoiled plan.

THE MADNESS OF YNYS MON

Ynys Mon, the holiest place in Britain, has been off-limits for over 400 years by order of the High Druid of Britain. Those who defy this ban risk madness and death.

BACKGROUND

In 61 AD Gaius Suetonius Paulinus, Roman Governor of Britannia, ordered the assault on Ynys Mon. The Legio XX Valeria Victrix, along with a cohort of cavalry auxiliaries from the Legio XIV Gemina, landed on the southeast and fought their way to the Holy Glade where the druids of 15 tribes had gathered, many of whom were accompanying their High Druid. Under the Eye of the Great Red Dragon itself, the Romans slaughtered the druids and their companions, and the power of British druidry was broken. Blaise, who was the High Druid of Britain at the time, pronounced a ban on the island, leaving it as a monument to the dead. His successor Merlin still enforces this edict.

Thanks to the High Druids' ban, Ynys Mon keeps what it has. The spirits of the druids the Romans killed remain here, as are those who sacrificed their lives to gain revenge along with the spirits of the Romans upon whom that vengeance was enacted. Blaise's edict closed the gates of the Otherworld on the island, meaning no spirit or discorporated soul can reach its final destination; and while on the island, all spirits have the Recurring Trait (Mythras, page 138). However, being "killed" is a harrowing experience for the spirits, and it has unhinged the minds of spirits who have suffered it again and again in the past four centuries.

The spirits on Ynys Mon are locked in perpetual battle with one another. The haunts of the Romans do battle with the spirits of the British druids and the ghosts of the grove-guardians. All the nature spirits native to Ynys Mon are also trapped, along with a multitude of other spirits who were with the druids at the ceremony. There may even be the dreams of one or two minor gods that the desperate druids summoned when Paulinus attacked.

hook

The characters deliberately going to Ynys Mon must be willing to defy Merlin, have his permission, or be ignorant of his edict. All druids know that the Sacred Isle is off-limits; non-druid characters know this on a successful Lore (Britain) or a Very Easy Lore (Gwynedd) roll.

The main motivations for visiting Ynys Mon are either to deliver something to the island or retrieve something from the island. Some examples include the following:

- Ynys Mon is a highly effective trap for a spirit that the characters cannot destroy because it is too powerful and/or has the Recurring Trait.

- An exquisite form of revenge against a hated enemy would be to cause their death on Ynys Mon. Their discorporated soul cannot achieve peace in the Otherworld and they would likely become a wraith, trapped there forever.

- Information or an artefact possessed by the ancient druids — or even the Romans — might be vital to the characters' current quest. For example, it is rumoured the Hamper of Garanhir (one of the Treasures of Britain) was hidden on Ynys Mon and may be there still.

- A desperate fugitive from the characters might take their chances on Ynys Mon. They may not fully comprehend the danger or may be equipped to deal with them (for example, a druid).

Merlin would only send characters to the island for a momentous reason, for example, to retrieve one of the Treasures of Britain. He insists a druid accompany them: if the characters do not have a druid amongst their number, he assigns one to babysit them for the trip.

The characters might accidentally arrive on the island, due to a storm or shipwreck. They quickly learn that leaving the island is much harder than arriving here (see details below).

This adventure seed presents the situation on Ynys Mon and the struggle for characters to leave, and is not a trivial undertaking.

ACTION & EVENTS

When the characters step foot on Ynys Mon, they find a landscape left to go wild for centuries. The ruins of long-abandoned settlements are overgrown with vegetation. There is fresh water and wild forage; the feral descendants of goats, pigs, and cattle roam the landscape along with the usual complement of wild animals. Those areas particularly thick with Haunts —the south-western and south-eastern coasts — have stunted and twisted vegetation, poisoned by the spiritual miasma that saps vitality from the plants and drives away animals. Characters may witness one of the ghostly battles playing out a fight that took place generations ago.

Leaving the island through mundane means is impossible without the help of the island's spirits. Ynys Mon is only a kilometre offshore at its furthest point, building a raft may seem a reasonable escape plan (though there are no usable materials like tools or rope to scavenge from the centuries-old ruins). However, the spirits make the mainland unattainable and hidden in fog. The spirits of the mist prevent navigation and cause befuddlement and confusion, spirits of the water currents turn around any vessel so that they face back towards shore, and so forth.

It does not take long before an ancestor spirit uses its Discorporate Spirit Ability to drag all the characters into the

World of Spirits. This druid spirit is probably of the same tribe as one or more of the characters, and its purpose is to communicate with the newcomers. The once-human spirit hungers for knowledge of its people. The landscape here is similar but all sensations are more vivid, and the influence of the Red Dragon is more evident. The baleful white eye of the White Dragon that usually dominates the Spirit World is half-lidded on Ynys Mon, casting everything in long shadows. The earth seems to flex and swell with the breathing of the Red Dragon upon which they stand, and the pattern of its scales are present on every leaf and stem. Most of the non-human spirits here have a dragonish mien.

A clock starts ticking when the characters cross the threshold into the World of Spirits: the characters must find a way to return to the World of Men before their neglected bodies die of thirst. The spirit that brought them here is unapologetic for its selfish actions; it tells them that each of the two camps of spirits on the island have a means for the characters to get back to their bodies.

The Druidic Spirits

Upon their death by Roman swords, many of the druids at the Battle of Ynys Mon, used to dealing with the World of Spirits, successfully completed the transformation into an ancestor spirit. While aware of their fate, they often forget that they are dead and have lost all track of time. The High Druids are eager for news of the World of Men and may be amazed at recent history. They remember Merlin, but only as a young lad not yet apprenticed to Blaise. Lesser druids and ordinary mortals became Haunts instead, retaining little of their personalities and memories and subjugated by the self-aware spirits.

The British spirits are divided between several inland villages, the largest of which are each ruled by the spirit of a High Druid:

- Llanfechell is the home to High Druid Gunovarus and other spirits of the Carvetii tribe. Near to the village are three slender columns of stone, each two metres high and arranged in a perfect triangle. In the centre of the stones is the Boar of the Twentieth, a hollow statue of gold, which was the standard of the Roman legion. Gunovarus and Mandubracis have a long-standing hatred of one another that harks back to their training under Aedd Mawr. Gunovarus is besotted with Saira but has never dared to mention this to her.

- Hen Blas is a dolmen made of three titanic boulders. The two upright stones are roughly conical in shape and over four metres high, with a flat capstone bridging the two. Nearby, Aedd Mawr, High Druid of the Dumnonii, holds camp. At the time of his death, Aedd was the eldest of the High Druids on Ynys Mon and wants the others to declare him their leader so he can command the collected forces against the Romans.

- Bedd Branwen, where Verica of the Ordovices holds court, is a site sacred to the goddess Branwen. Located within a bowl-shaped depression sits a short menhir surrounded by curb stones. She has the largest contingent of druid spirits: 12 of her attendants accompanied her to Ynys Mon and they spend most their time in meditation around Branwen's stone. Like Aedd, Verica also desires to be leader of Ynys Mon's druids and believes her rival is too doddery to take on the role.

- Mandubracis, High Druid of the Catuvellauni, has claimed Din Sylwy as his home. This hillfort is defended by drystone walls made of huge limestone blocks that were placed here by giants. Mandubracis supports his mentor Aedd Mawr; he has a plan to use the giants (elemental spirits of earth) to dam the River Braint and then release the waters in one go to flood the Roman camp. This has made him an enemy of Saira.

- High Druid Teuhant of the Silures occupies the wooded hills of the island's northwest. Deep in the primal forest is Garreg Hir, a standing stone of pink quartzite. At its foot is a darker slab-shaped stone stained even darker by the blood of captured Romans, whose spirits bleed just as well as their bodies would. Teuhant is fiercely independent; he does not want either Aedd or Verica to be elected as their leader, especially Verica whose tribe is opposed to his own. Teuhant is supportive of Saira; he likes the ruthlessness of the druidess and her bloodthirsty goddess.

- The source of the River Braint that runs past the Holy Grove is Llyn Llwydiarth. The lakeside is home to a group of druidesses native to Ynys Mon. Lead by Saira, these are guardians of the Holy Grove dedicated to the serpent goddess Braint. The grove guardians are trained in battle magic and fight naked except for the snakes that entwine their bodies. Saira will not allow any disrespect to her patron goddess. She is wary of Gunovarus, who acts oddly in her presence.

These may not be the only spirits of High Druids on Ynys Mon, but are the most easily accessible since they control large congregations of other spirits. The druid spirits have a ritual called Opening the Eye, which returns discorporated yet still unsundered souls (i.e., those with living bodies) to the World of Men. However, conducting this ritual requires three High Druids to stand at the three stones at Llanfechell and currently none of the High Druids are willing to cooperate with any of the others. The characters must negotiate the politics of the six camps: the key alliance to make is between Gunovarus and Saira who together as a pair can then team up with Aedd, Teuhant, or Verica to make up the trio needed to complete the ritual.

The Ghost Legion (see below) has exploratores — scouts tasked with keeping an eye on enemy movements — throughout Ynys Mon, so the visits of the characters to the various camps does not go unnoticed. The characters have a chance to spot the scouts, but if they do not stop them all, then the Roman Legate learns someone is trying to coordinate the British forces and musters his army for an assault.

The Ghost Legion

The soul of every soldier who killed a druid was drawn back here by the druids' death curse, whether the soldier died on Ynys Mon or survived the battle and died elsewhere. The Roman Legate who lead the army in life continues to do so in death. His given name is long forgotten, even by himself, and he has become a powerful wraith. His men are mostly Haunts driven by duty; there are more than a few who have become aware of their plight and driven mad through centuries of isolation. The Ghost Legion is at one-third strength (about 300 soldiers) and may have some Roman tutelary spirits associated with it.

The Roman spirits are camped out at the Holy Grove at Bryn Celli Ddu, which contains the Eye of the Great Red Dragon, a well that bridges the Worlds. A discorporated soul that climbs into the well and literally prises open the eyelid of the sleeping dragon is caught in its gaze and reunited with its body in the World of Men. The Eye of the Great Red Dragon is well guarded and the Legate won't provide access to the well without first gaining a service from the characters.

The standard of the Legio XX was lost during the fight with the druids. It is a boar made of gold, hung with the medals and honours received by the legion. The Legate offers them access to the Eye of the Great Red Dragon if the characters retrieve the standard from the druids. The Romans suspect one of the High Druids has the Boar and their scouts can give an account of the various camps and their leaders. The characters may choose to infiltrate one of the druid camps and gather information, or use subterfuge to check each one in turn. The Boar is currently amongst the stones at Llanfechell; to retrieve it, the characters must evade or defeat the spirits that High Druid Gunovarus has placed to guard it. The stones are guarded at all times by a pack of predator spirits in the shape of wolves and watched over by nature (raven) spirits. Furthermore, the Boar itself has been cursed: anyone carrying it has their Movement Rate reduced by five metres per round.

CLIMAX

If the characters plan to return to their bodies via the ritual of the High Druids, then as the ritual commences, the amassed Romans begin their attack. The characters must keep the Ghost Legion occupied for the time it takes to complete the ritual. They could lead the British spirits in a counter-attack using the Battle rules (Mythic Britain, page 179) or else harry them with guerrilla tactics.

If instead the characters successfully return the Boar to the Roman Legate, he insists on a ceremony to reward them with military honours before they pass through the Eye of the Great Red Dragon. At this ceremony, the Roman Legate plans to betray the characters by ordering the honour guard to attack during the presentation. The characters must fight their way to the Eye.

The characters may end up destroying the Roman Legate. Without a commander, the Ghost Legion slips back into its stereotypic behaviour, providing temporary surcease of the endless war while the wraith reforms its essence. If the characters still wanted to use the Eye of the Great Red Dragon, this would be the best time, since sneaking into the Roman camp unobserved is a lot simpler without the Legate commanding the troops.

If the characters leave the Spirit World (by whatever means) in the presence of the Roman Legate, he attempts to possess one of them as they leave. If the wraith wins a Special Effect or manages to defeat his foe, then he rides their soul out of the World of Spirits and escape the prison of Ynys Mon. The Games Master might want to keep this Spirit Combat private between themselves and the player of the character affected, so that the other players do not know it is happening.

CONSEQUENCES

If the characters can win their way back to their bodies, then the spirits of the land withdraw their obfuscating powers from the island and allow them to escape the island altogether.

If the Roman Legate successfully possessed someone, the wraith remains in Covert Possession in the first instance as it watches and learns about the world. However, it seeks the downfall of the Britons in general and druids in particular, and may begin to use the character's body to secretly bring these plans about. It would be particularly dangerous to bring the Legate into Arthur's court. A druid may well be able to detect the spirit squatting around the character's soul (Merlin certainly would), and the wraith takes steps to avoid druids altogether.

The souls of characters whose bodies die on Ynys Mon are trapped there. Characters who survive but who lose all their Magic Points (or Tenacity, if using that mechanic) while on Ynys Mon are driven mad. This affliction takes many forms, some of which might mimic Conditions such as Mania, Hallucinations, or Paralysis. This state is permanent, although a Heal Mind Miracle can remove it.

The Head of Bran the Blessed

The Head of Bran the Blessed is a fabled relic of pagan Britain, perhaps as powerful as the Thirteen Treasures. Bran was the brother of the god Manawydan and was the High King of Britain in the Time of Heroes.

BACKGROUND

Bran, also known as Bedigeidfran or "Bran the Blessed," ruled Britain from Arddlech in present-day Dunodion. His sister Branwen married King Matholwch of Ireland. When word came to Bran that Matholwch had mistreated Branwen, King Bran declared war on Ireland. The battle did not go well for the British troops. Bran had given Matholwch the Cauldron of Resurrection as a wedding present, and the Irish king used it to restore life to his slain warriors, giving him an endless supply. Bran knew the only way to defeat him was to destroy the cauldron, and he alone knew its flaw. The Cauldron was meant for the dead: a living man placed inside would break the enchantment. Bran used his magic to disguise himself as an Irishman's corpse and Matholwch duly him placed inside. With a mighty crack, the Cauldron of Resurrection shattered into pieces, but just as the Cauldron gave life to the dead, it took life from the living and Bran was slain. Without the Cauldron, Matholwch's advantage was lost and the British eventually prevailed but the losses on both sides were outstanding — only five Irish women and seven British men survived the battle. The seven Britons took the Head of Bran and the remaining pieces of the Cauldron back to the Island of the Mighty, leaving the women to repopulate Ireland. The pieces of the Cauldron were given to the High Druid of Britain and were later bolted back together to make the Cauldron of Dyrnwch.

Seven guardians (possibly those same survivors) still care for the Urddawl Ben ("Noble Head"), as it has become known. The Head retains the power of speech and knows everything that is known by at least two people (so it does not know a person's secrets unless revealed to or discovered by another; similarly, it does not know the future). However, Bran's answers are either brief and plain or complete but in the form of a riddle. After answering a question, the Head sleeps for 1d3 years, during which time it cannot be woken.

book

The Guardians of the Urddawl Ben do not permit any mortal king to own the Head, but occasionally they allow petitioners to put a single question to it — five people are known to have consulted the oracle in the last 10 years. Merlin or the leader of their faction might contract the characters to ask it a particular vexing question. Alternatively, the characters might have their own question in need of an answer.

ACTION & EVENTS

Before they can ask their question, the characters need to find the Head. They then must make the perilous journey to its place of concealment and persuade the Guardians — through force or diplomacy — to give them access.

As an added complication, making enquiries about the Head alerts the Blackshield Irish. Connor mac Eird considers the Urddawl Ben to be the property of his clan, and it would earn him significant status were he to regain it — perhaps enough to allow him to return from exile.

Looking for the Head

The Guardians move the Urddawl Ben periodically in order to keep it hidden. However, they have become complacent and are moving the Head on a regular cycle. If the characters discover where the Head has been recently, they can make a reasonable guess at where it is now. The Games Master can make as much or as little of this mystery as desired. Their patron might already know where the previous petitioners of the Urddawl Ben went and simply tell them the information below. At the other extreme, the characters may have to visit some or all of the people below and ask them.

- Morgana (Mythic Britain, page 202) consulted it 7 years ago after Mordred was slain. At this time, it was in Bedd y Idwal.
- A peasant called Bledri consulted it four years ago, when it was in Cader Idris. Famously, he stumbled upon it and squandered his question on a banal topic — but he did find his lost sheep.
- Owain ap Einion sought out the Head five years ago before the birth of his son; he claims to have failed to find it, but this is a convenient deceit to save face amongst the Christian Einionydd. He located the Head at Meini Hirion.
- Morcanwg (page 15) consulted it 10 years ago when it was in Meini Hirion.
- Bleiddud ap Meirion consulted it 8 years ago after the death of his brother, when it was in Cader Idris.

Apart from Bledri, none of the petitioners reveal what question they asked the Head. If the locations are arranged in chronological order, the characters can make a reasonable guess that the Urddawl Ben currently resides at Bedd y Idwal.

The Blackshield Irish

Unless the characters have been very careful with their enquiries regarding the Head of Bran the Blessed, Connor mac Eird becomes aware that they are also looking for it and sends his own band of adventurers to intercept the characters and obtain the Head for him. The Blackshield Irish want the characters to succeed in finding the Head where they themselves have failed, but they want to prevent the characters from asking it a question. If this occurs after "The Quarrelling Princes" adventure (page 27) and Saoirse and Tiorrach survived, then these two lead the Irish band.

The Games Master can use the Blackshield Irish in a number of ways, which depends very much on the status of the characters and any prior interaction with Connor's pirates:

- As antagonists, dogging the characters' steps at every turn.
- As competitors, racing the characters to the prize.
- As allies, joining forces with the characters with a potential double-cross at the last moment, stealing the Head away before the characters ask their question.

Even if the characters manage to ask their question, the Irish still have orders to retrieve the Head; Connor considers it to be his and three years is not so long to wait.

The Giant's Grave

Bedd y Idwal, or "the grave of Idwal," lies amongst the jagged peaks of the Eryri Mountains. The characters need good instructions to find the hidden valley, and the weather could further compound the challenge. This area of the mountains is home to the giant Idven Gawr, son of Idwal Gawr, whose grave they seek (all giants have the family name of "Gawr," it simply means "giant"). Idven promised the Guardians he would help protect the Head of Bran; he is no friend to humans but does not consider them vermin or food like some.

Idven's skin is the colour of the surrounding rocks, mottled and textured like stone. He is bare-chested and wears "stone mail" trews of his own invention, consisting of plates of slate sewn onto goatskin. Idven's statistics are those of a standard giant (Mythras, page 245), although he has 5 Armour Points on his abdomen and leg Hit Locations thanks to his unusual armour. Due to his skin and clothing, when he is in an area with lots of exposed rock, he benefits from the Camouflaged Creature Ability and his Stealth is 62%. He can also throw his voice, as per the Ventriloquism Folk Magic Spell. He is terrified of water, since Idwal drowned in the lake that now marks his grave.

When the characters first encounter Idven, he is camouflaged against a scree slope in a valley. He projects his voice to the other side of the valley and commands the characters to turn back, his booming voice causing some stones to dislodge and skitter to the valley floor (a warning that the ground is not wholly stable). He does his best to dissuade the characters from continuing onwards, using threats if necessary. If they spot him, he is more overtly aggressive, lifting a boulder above his head and roaring. If the characters hold their nerve, he does not attack — the characters likely look like they can handle themselves and he owes no allegiance to the Guardians of the Head other than a rather vague promise to scare people off.

If the characters offer Idven a toll, he'll take advantage of the idea, demanding goats to eat: there's a wild herd nearby, and to prolong this episode further, the Games Master can put the goats under the protection of a gwyll (page 26). Idven might even offer directions to the Bedd y Idwal if the characters ask him nicely; he gives them a carved stone and asks them to lay it at his father's feet.

If met with aggression, Idven sends a small avalanche of loose shingle down on the characters from his position on the slope and then rolls boulders down the hill at them, aiming first at those with missile weapons. He would prefer not to engage in melee, although his stone-covered clothing offers him ample protection.

Bedd y Idwal is a spectacular hanging valley, steep sides leading to a semi-circular wall of rock with a lake at its base. Idwal's gigantic grave juts out into the lake, a narrow causeway terminating in a protruding island where the giant's head would be buried. The island is big enough for a few trees and a small meadow, with a couple of buildings that house the Guardians and the Shrine of the Head.

CLIMAX

The seven Guardians of the Head share their names of the seven survivors of the battle against Matholwch (see the "Background"), although these may be pseudonyms rather than them being the same seven people. The Guardians are all warriors and druids (although typically specialising in one

OTHER RESTING PLACES

Cader Idris ("the chair of Idris") is a mountain in Meirionydd that is reputed to be the hunting-ground of Arawn, God of the Underworld. Those who sleep on the slopes of the mountain at Samhain wake up either raving mad or a gifted poet.

Meini Hirion ("the tall stones") is Gwynedd's most spectacular stone circle. It stands on the headland of Penmaenmawr, close to a prehistoric trackway and three other stone circles. The circle has around 30 stones and a portalled entrance guarded by two stones each side.

of these professions). In addition, each one has a different supernatural power:

- Manaw can move as swiftly as the wind, fast enough even to run over water.
- Taliesin Ben Beirdd ("Chief of Bards") has a silver tongue and can compel others to tell the truth.
- Pryderi ap Pwyll cannot be killed; he does not suffer Major Wounds and regenerates lesser injuries.
- Heilyn ap Gwyn can turn invisible for as long as he can hold his breath.
- Gluneu Eil Taran can crush anything he can get between his hands.
- Ynawc has senses so acute that he can see grass grow from a kilometre away and hear the wool grow on a sheep's back.
- Grudyen ap Muryel can carry any weight he can get on his back.

If the characters try to take the Head by force, they have a fight on their hands. Ynawc almost certainly senses the characters' approach and warns the others. He stands on a high pole, which gives him a commanding view of the valley, and is armed with a sling and does not suffer Distance Penalties thanks to his power. Manaw, Gluneu, Grudyen, and Pryderi are the chief warriors of the Guardians, and they can easily defend the causeway that leads to the Shrine of the Head, since it allows only two warriors to face them in melee at a time, leaving the other two to prevent those who brave the icy waters of the lake to swim around them.

The characters do not have to fight the Guardians. If given the chance, Taliesin speaks to the characters, partly to find out how they located the Head's hiding place, but partly to

negotiate terms. If the characters can convince him that their cause is just, then the Guardians allow the question to be asked. The characters could even ally with the Guardians against the Blackshield Irish who want to seize possession of the Urddawl Ben.

The Head is kept in a small shrine decorated with motifs of waves and horses. An embossed golden shield bearing the image of Branwen sits opposite a plinth carved from a tree trunk, upon which there is an unremarkable skull, brown with age. This, however, is a decoy to prevent thieves — the real Head is encased inside the hollow plinth. The myths give Bran a gigantic stature and his head is two metres tall. Sagging, partly rotted and partly mummified flesh still hangs on the skull and the hair and beard are tangled like a bramble thicket. The eyelids snap open to reveal eyeballs like cloudy jelly, and its slimy tongue flops out of its mouth and wets its lips before it speaks.

CONSEQUENCES

Bran's voice is deep and sonorous and can be heard by everyone within earshot (like the Voice Folk Magic spell). The Head demands to know why it has been disturbed, prompting the characters to pose their question, which must be uttered in a single breath (this restriction is well known to druids and bards). If possible, Bran's answer should be in verse, even if it is simple doggerel. Bran does not deliberately twist the meaning of the question, but his answers are occasionally brief and unhelpful.

For instance, if the characters are here to ask about the Coat of Beisrydd, the Head might answer in the following way:

*"The king of druids seeks Padarn's coat
that the druid king hid in Aywell's Throat;
the snake has it not, and nor does the fish,
but the cave's maid yields it in exchange for a wish."*

Merlin can easily interpret the first part of this utterance: if he is the king of druids, then Mawgaus must be the Druid King, and "Aywell's Throat" must be the Caves of Aywell in the territory of the Circind Votadini. The last lines give the characters a clue where to look when they get to the Caves of the Circind.

After speaking his answer, the Head lapses into a deep slumber from which it cannot be awakened for 1d3 Years. The guardians usually move the Urddawl Ben immediately after a question has been put to it.

If the characters did not battle with the Guardians on the way to the Shrine of the Head, then the Games Master might want to have them fight their way free. Their opponents are most likely the Blackshield Irish, understandably upset that the characters got to the Head first. They seek to take the Head back to their prince and the Guardians might ask for help.

Appendices
Maps & Pronunciation

If you want to attempt Welsh pronunciation for the people and places in this book, here is some guidance. Note the following:

- "ll" is pronounced roughly as a rolled "cloo" sound, here represented as "cl."
- "ch" is pronounced as in Scottish "loch," not as in English "church."
- Syllables in UPPER case are stressed.

Afallach (ah-VA-CLAACH)
Afflogion (aff-LOG-ee-on)
Afloyg (AV-loig)
Arfon (AR-von)
Aula (EYE-la)
Benlli (BEN-clee)
Bleiddud (BLAY-thid)
Cadwallon Lawhir (kad-WAH-clon LAW-heer)
Ceredig (keh-REH-dig)
Ceredigydd (keh-reh-DIG-ith)
Connor mac Eird (CON-nor mac AIR-D) [Irish]
Cunedda (kin-ETH-a)
Dafyn (DAH-vin)
Deithlyn (DAYTH-lin)
Dinas Affaraon (DIN-as af-a-RAH-on)
Dogfeil (DOG-veil)
Dogfeilion (dog-VAY-lee-on)
Dunodion (din-OD-ee-on)
Dwynwen (DWIN-wen)
Dylan (DUL-an)
Dynod (DUN-od)
Ederyn (eh-DEH-rin)
Ederynion (eh-deh-RIN-ee-on)
Einion (ay-NEE-on)
Einionydd (ay-nee-ON-ith)

Eithne (ETH-ne) [Irish]
Elnaw (EL-now)
Gluneu Eil Taran (GLIN-ay ale TAR-an)
Grudyen ap Muryel (GRID-yen ap MIR-yel)
Gwaelod (GW-EYE-lod)
Gwawl (GW-OWL, rhymes with 'owl')
Gwyddno (GWITH-no)
Gwynedd (GWIN-eth)
Gwrin (GEAR-in)
Heilyn ap Gwyn (HAY-lin ap GWIN)
Manaw (MAH-now)
Meddyf (METH-eev)
Maeldaf (MILE-dav)
Meirion (may-REE-on)
Meirionydd (may-ree-ON-ith)
Meredith (meh-RED-ith)
Mererid (meh-REH-rid)
Morcanwg (mor-KAN-oog)
Morfran (MOR-vran)
Morvan (MOR-van)
Osfael (OS-vile)
Owain Ddantgwyn (OH-wine THANT-gwin)
Pryderi ap Pwyll (pri-DER-ee ap PWI-CL)
Rhos (HROS)
Rhufoniog (hree-VON-ee-og)
Rhwfon (HROO-von)
Saoirse (SUR-sha) [Irish]
Seithenyn Hen (say-THEN-in HEN)
Taliesin Ben Beirdd (tal-ee-ESS-in ben BEAR-TH)
Tiorrach (CHUR-roch) [Irish]
Ynawc (UN-owk)

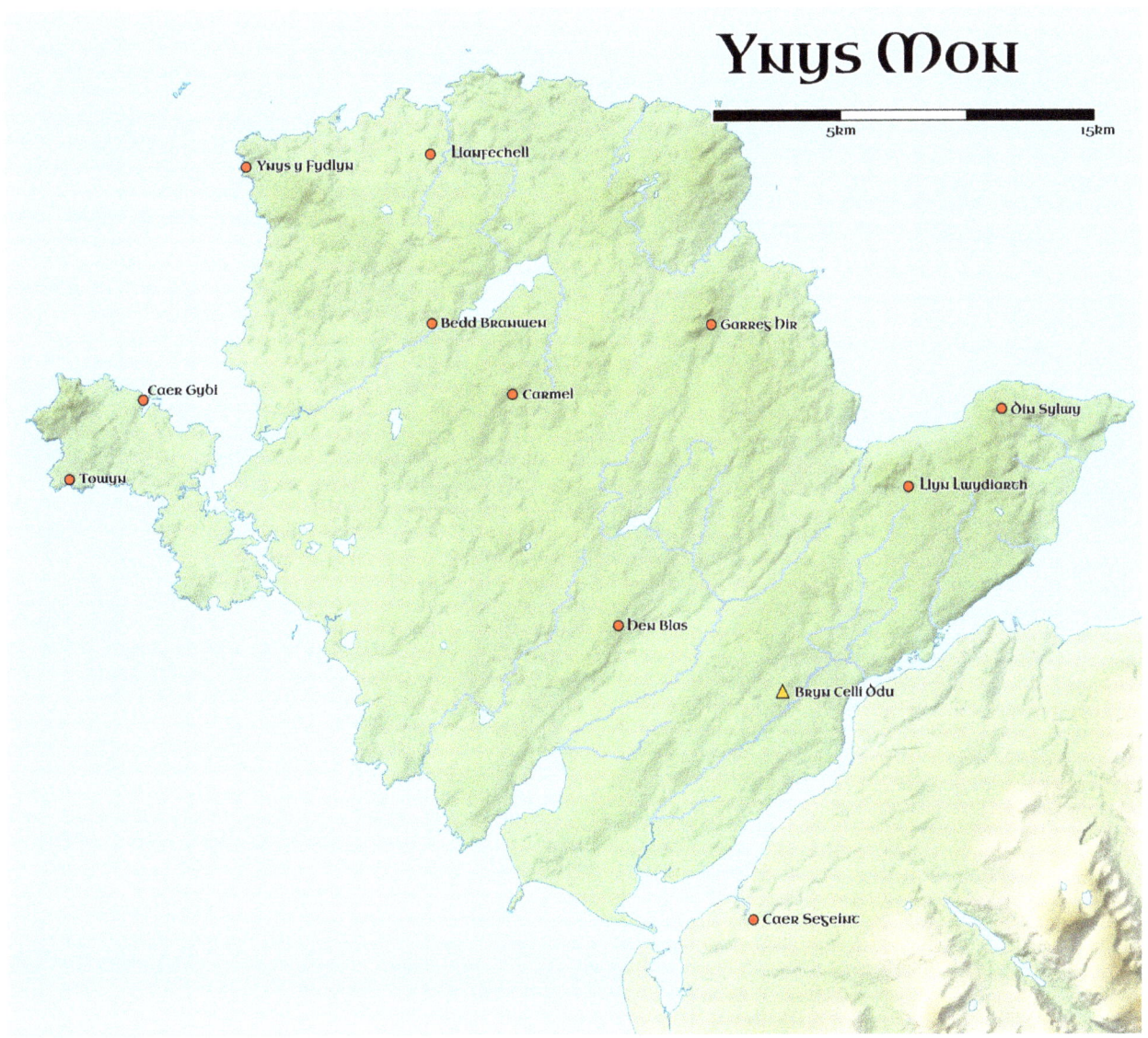

www.ingramcontent.com/pod-product-compliance
Ingram Content Group UK Ltd.
Pitfield, Milton Keynes, MK11 3LW, UK
UKHW051449220525
458812UK00005B/13